The Supernova Advisor

The Supernova Advisor

CROSSING THE INVISIBLE BRIDGE TO EXCEPTIONAL CLIENT SERVICE AND CONSISTENT GROWTH

Rob Knapp

John Wiley & Sons, Inc.

Published by John Wiley & Sons, Inc., Hoboken, New Jersey.
Published simultaneously in Canada.

Wiley Bicentennial Logo: Richard J. Pacifico

For general information on our other products and services or for technical support, please contact our Customer Care Department within the United States at (800) 762-2974, outside the United States at (317) 572-3993 or fax (317) 572-4002.

Wiley also publishes its books in a variety of electronic formats. Some content that appears in print may not be available in electronic formats. For more information about Wiley products, visit our Web site at www.wiley.com.

Library of Congress Cataloging-in-Publication Data:

Knapp, Rob, 1946-
    The supernova advisor : crossing the invisible bridge to exceptional client service and consistent growth/Rob Knapp.
        p.   cm.
    Includes index.
    ISBN 978-0-470-24927-7 (cloth)
        1. Investment advisor-client relationships.   2. Customer relations.
    3. Management.   4. Leadership.   I. Title.
    HG4621.K64   2008
    658.8'12—dc22

                                                                    2007034473

Printed in the United States of America
20   19   18

*This book is dedicated to my wife, Marcia,
and our children, Courtney and Christopher.
Their patience and faith kept my travels
from becoming absence. Their enthusiasm
inspires me almost as much as their love
nourishes me. The rest of my life is dedicated
to returning everything they have given.*

Contents

Foreword

When Rob Knapp asked me to contribute the forward on his Supernova book, I agreed straightaway. But before we go forward, let me take you back a bit. I'm considered somewhat of an expert on helping leaders create changes in people—changes that result in a better bottom line for their organization. At least, that's the work I get paid to do.

It's no secret that getting people to change themselves, not because they have to, but because they want to, defines the word *leadership*. The drama plays out when a leader is coaching others to willingly get out of their comfort zone, jump into their learning zone, and start to think and behave in new or different ways. This is the most difficult assignment that any leader can tackle, whether as a parent, teacher, minister, priest, rabbi, boss, or friend. When that's happening, change is happening, and it's a leaders job to spark those happenings.

Rob Knapp is one of those rare leaders.

Rob and his teams have gotten a PhD in the hard knocks school of leaders leading change. Better yet, they've transformed what they've learned into a powerful change system called Supernova. This is a can't-fail change system that anyone who's willing to do the work can accomplish. How do I know? I saw it happen, saw it with my own eyes, saw it big time, and saw it create fabulous results for all the players in the game.

Okay, *now* we can move forward. I want to take you forward into your future so you can see what I saw.

I saw Rob and his teams leading groups of stubbornly entrenched people to willingly transform themselves by turning to a new path of future possibility that truly set them free. It's the path of the Supernova advantage.

And that's only half of the story. As a client of one of these Supernova teams, I experienced all the Supernova customer benefits that set *me* free. Okay, you got it; I'm a huge Rob Knapp fan, just as you'll be by the time you get to middle of Chapter 1 in this book. Rob makes you want to follow him because it will set you free—free to become the most successful and fulfilled advisor coach in your niche of the world. I can sum up in two words what you'll want to do after you've read the last page: *Clone him.*

Rob Knapp is a rare person who can lead a traditional command-and-control organization through genuine sustainable change. And when that person is neither the commander nor the controller of that organization, it's beyond rare. It's remarkable. It's in the realm of phenomenal.

Look, my business *is* change—studying it, coaching it, inhabiting it, and inhaling in very personal terms—and I've never encountered anyone like Rob Knapp. In the dictionary of Larry Wilson, look up *change agent* and you'll see Rob's picture. Look up *Supernova* and you'll see a couple of thousand more people who successfully changed the way they work because, through Rob's teaching, they changed how they even thought about work. They weren't *told* to change; they changed because Rob and his teams showed them an idea powerful enough to overcome all the negative barriers to change.

The role of any leader is to bring about change, not because change itself is inherently better than the status quo, but look out the window and notice that our whole world is changing. Staying put is a recipe for failure, so it's a leader's prime responsibility to get others on a better path to success and fulfillment. It's then they'll want to develop themselves so they too can become leaders in the rapidly changing cultural landscapes we all inhabit. Rob's not the first guy to figure this out. In fact, the need to continually evolve with, or ahead of, the business environment is becoming a basic survival strategy in every leader's tool kit.

So why, then, is change so hard to execute, and how did Rob and his team accomplish it? The answer awaits you, but I'll offer this preview: Rob realized that leading people to change is an emotional challenge, not merely an intellectual one. When Rob invited the financial advisors of Merrill Lynch to follow him onto the invisible bridge, he didn't hire teams of hotshot outsiders. He tapped into the emotions of the people within the Merrill culture, and refocused them with imagination, intuition, and, yes, intelligence. There were some very rational, left-brained reasons why adopting Supernova made sense, and Rob integrated them within an argument as emotionally powerful as it was intellectually sound.

The adoption of Supernova was a phenomenon in another way, too, equally as compelling. It arose from the field, where the problems were felt and the answers were forthcoming when true leaders give expectations, permission, and protection to their followers to do so.

In most organizations, attempting change is driven too much from the top. Solutions are fashioned not from collaborating with the field, but by pushing down "do what you're told to do" from those furthest from the customer. No invisible bridge, just planks to walk and orders to follow. The Supernova story has a totally different look and feel and produces more results with less effort and far less stress.

It's a story of the people—the little people—trusting each other and leading each other to the promised land of fruits and honey.

All that being said, Supernova wasn't the focal point of reorganization. There were no special project teams pulled away from their day-to-day jobs. The people at the center of Supernova simply volunteered to help spread the word about a better way to serve their clients and grow their business. Why? Their visibility certainly wasn't going to help them advance through the organization, and there were no bonuses waiting on the other end of a successful implementation.

The people who preached Supernova simply did so for the good of their peers. Why do soldiers fight? Not for a flag, but for each other. Not to overdo it, but this group led this collaborative change process for one another. And, I'm delighted to report, for their clients—clients like me. Now that's different!

As I said, I'm a loyal client of a Merrill team that adopted and still practices Supernova. They execute the model expertly, and they continue to grow, and so do I. I love to recommend them. They treat me as though I'm one of their best clients, and it's not because I have tens of millions parked with them. It's because of their Supernova mind-set.

You'll learn all about the magic of the model as you read Rob's book.

As a client of a Supernova team, I really relish the service and the investment expertise. I have a financial plan based on my life plan; my investments are built around that financial plan, and I get a phone call every month, four reviews and two in person. I also appreciate that my team has time for me if I have a problem, and it is resolved quickly. This is very different than my previous experience. I am eager to refer business to my financial advisor team. They, too, treat me as though I am one of their best clients. I know why now. It's because of Supernova. And Supernova is because of Rob Knapp.

I'll never forget watching Rob as he retold the story of Indiana Jones standing on the cliff, torn between his fear of falling and his trust that the bridge would hold him. Trust won out for Indiana Jones, and for the thousands of professionals who crossed the bridge. Rob's gift then, and now, is that he knows that trust is the glue that advances all of us as professionals and enriches us as humans.

So *The Supernova Advisor* is as close to cloning Rob as you can get. His genius is in here, as well as his creativity and generosity. Don't just read this book—devour each and every practice as though your future depends on it, because it does. Cross the bridge, and be sure to bring your customers along with you. When everybody wins, the world *is* a better place. Thank Rob and yourself for making a difference in so many lives. So Be It!

LARRY WILSON
September 2007

Larry Wilson is widely considered one of the foremost thinkers, speakers, and doers in the business world today. He founded two premier companies:

Wilson Learning Corporation (1965), a more than $50 million training and research organization; and Pecos River Learning (1985), a change management and leadership development organization. These companies Larry founded have carved new territories in how we think about business, customers, and ourselves. Larry's newest venture is called Wilson Collaborative, a new business model for new thinking leaders.

As an author, his writings are world renowned. In 1984, he co-authored the best seller The One-Minute Sales Person *(Morrow, 1984), which sold over one million copies. His other best-selling books include:* Changing the Game: The New Way to Sell *(Simon & Schuster, 1987) and* Stop Selling, Start Partnering *(John Wiley & Sons, 1997). His latest book,* Play to Win! Choosing Growth over Fear in Work and Life *(Bard Press, 1998), was selected Best Business Book for 1999 by* ForeWord *magazine as well as winning the prestigious Benjamin Franklin Award for Best Business Book for 1999. He is a Senior Fellow at the College of Education & Human Development, University of Minnesota. In May 2005, Northland College granted Larry an honorary PhD in business.*

Acknowledgments

Supernova was created in the rarest of spaces, a place without ego, a region where the personal pronoun "I" yielded to a larger purpose. Supernova was brought to life by a group of people, to help a large group serve an even larger group. We created a new way to work, and grow, and serve. Here, I honor their courage and celebrate their success.

To chronicle my appreciation, Supernova's initial practitioners are the best place to begin. We called them "Pioneers" because they were truly the first to venture into this new territory. They took the leap of faith and stepped onto the invisible bridge first—George Kempf, Tony Singh, Jim McEnerney, and Hagood Ellison were Supernova's most persuasive spokespeople, not because of what they said but because of what they *accomplished*. You'll read some of their stories in the chapters ahead.

Jim Walker, the Chief Administrative Officer of Merrill Lynch, helped us develop the solid footing that Supernova rose from. His contribution to "8 Steps to Success" was Supernova's genesis. Jim did all the original research to support what we felt intuitively. He brought researchers from Harvard and MIT into the conversation and invited them to poke and probe at Supernova, to test it in laboratories, and tell us the truth about what we had created. As CAO, Jim gave us the executive air support we needed, and he stood with us on stage at that very first rollout meeting in Boston. His very presence said simply, "I believe." And I am very grateful.

Jeff Ransdell did more than give the model its wonderfully appropriate name. He also gave us the confidence to take Supernova on the road to other Merrill Lynch districts. He knew that peer-to-peer transmission was the only way this disruptive idea could thrive. Jeff helped construct the core pieces of Supernova. He designed the spreadsheet and did the research that put the first hard ceiling on how many clients could take a seat on the first Supernova flights.

John Hesse deserves more than can be acknowledged here. Far more. He put in hundreds of hours developing the Supernova software and then trained Supernova tech teams across the country. He *was* the Supernova tech support department, and it's fitting that the software he created—that helped FAs simplify and justify their client segmentation decisions—is often called "The Hesse Report."

Jon Spafford's early insight that merely annuitizing the FA's business wasn't going to help it thrive. His idea to "automate" and "elevate" are still alive today in the Supernova advisor's organization and segmentation. Jon is an engineer of the advisory business, brilliant, visionary, and greatly appreciated.

Kim Firestone was Supernova's first and only full-time employee. And that doesn't come close to describing how central and essential she was to its success. No one else could manage the technology and the human personalities as well as Kim. She was a one-person training department. She stayed in the districts after the presentation team left and helped transform the enthusiasm into meaningful change. She was, and is, a force of nature whose energy sustained Supernova throughout its development.

James Gorman envisioned Supernova as integral to the Merrill Lynch strategy and allowed its early promise to prove itself in the FA teams across the country. His steady confidence was a source of strength for every member of the development team and every FA who took the step onto that bridge.

Andy Seig and Bob Sherman helped Supernova survive through their determination to help Merrill's client call center develop in both capacity and service capability. Without their advocacy, Supernova could not have succeeded on the scale that it did.

Karla Ransdell kept us focused on where Supernova's soul resided: planning. Her enthusiasm for the entire model energized us all.

Bob Dineen was the first one to suggest we take Supernova on the road. Did I say "suggest"? He nearly commanded us, and we're grateful that he did.

Before Supernova erupted and all we knew was our service was eroding and our clients were leaving, Jim Shoaf was a warrior for knowledge. His energy drove us deep into the structural issues at the core, and his continual challenges propelled us toward the solution that became Supernova.

Supernova puts the client associate in a leadership position on the team, so it's fitting that our own Supernova team had Kelly Carroll front and center. She was both a spokesperson from the stage during rollouts and a superb supporter for the teams implementing Supernova.

Darby Henley's firsthand understanding of accountability's power to transform a team was essential to developing the leadership components of Supernova. And Bob Johnson was the first to suggest that our Supernova principles created something greater than the sum of its parts when configured in the five-star constellation we see today.

Like all exceptional assistants, Mary Ann Urbancic's contributions can't be specifically identified because there simply aren't enough pages. Suffice it to say, she did about everything, every day. The more complex the challenge, the more calm competence she brought to it. Supernova is as much hers as it is anyone else's on these pages.

I learned long ago that the title of mentor should not be granted easily. Given the level that genuine mentors operate on, it's nearly a sacred title. Mentoring me now and throughout my career have been Richard Weylman, Larry Wilson, and Jim Loehr.

Richard helped me see the wisdom and elegance in Supernova's early emphasis on segmenting our clients and organizing our service. His mentorship then deepened as we discussed, and then presented, Supernova's acquisition component. Richard added immeasurable richness and impact by helping our FAs to present themselves as true brands. He was, and remains, ahead of his time.

Larry's restless brilliance has inspired me to challenge the status quo while simultaneously envisioning new pathways. His life of choosing growth over fear is true leadership embodied. He is a teacher of the highest order.

Jim's insights into reaching and sustaining peak performance have reshaped not only how I work, but how I live.

This book has been a collaboration nearly as enriching as Supernova itself, and several people deserve my gratitude. Julie Young is a spirited muse and a careful reader. I'm deeply appreciative of her continuing guidance and gently powerful wisdom. Greg Perry inhabits every page of this book. In our editorial partnership, he lifted Supernova out of my memory and helped me see it with fresh eyes and communicate it with renewed vigor.

My appreciation extends to every advisor and every team that brought this new way of working into their businesses. Each one stood on the edge of a canyon and took an exhilarating first step onto the invisible bridge of Supernova. This book is for them, and for every professional who follows them.

ROB KNAPP
September 2007

Stepping onto the Invisible Bridge

YOUR JOURNEY TOWARD THE EXCEPTIONAL

Some movies offer remarkably appropriate metaphors for the choices we make in our careers and lives. In *Indiana Jones and the Last Crusade,* Indy's quest to find the Holy Grail quickly becomes more than a professional obsession; it's a family emergency. His father is shot in the stomach by the Nazi protagonist, and his only hope for survival is a drink from the grail.

The Nazi tells Indy, "It's time to ask yourself what you believe."

Three tests stand between Indy and the grail chamber. After passing the first two with swashbuckling flair, Indy arrives at a test of faith. To reach the chamber that houses the grail, he must first cross to the other side of a 30-foot cavern. There is no bridge—at least no visible bridge. To step out is to literally take a leap of faith. And faith goes against everything he stands for as a rational, intellectual college professor.

In this book, you will be encouraged to take a leap of faith, too. It's a way of working that might run counter to what you've come to believe about your business, be it an investment advisory or another consultative, service-oriented profession. Along with firsthand accounts of people who have made the leap and are now succeeding in the best sense of the word, you're going to learn how to grow your business by deepening *what your business means* to your clients.

But I left you hanging from the cliff—back to the movie.

Following the instructions in his father's diary, Indy begins to step across the cavern and into the void. To his amazement, his foot lands on solid ground. A bridge existed, but its rocky texture perfectly matched the facing wall of the cavern, *so that it was invisible from Indy's perspective.* Like certain ideas that surprise us with their simplicity while energizing us with their power, the bridge was there all along.

There is an invisible bridge before you now. This bridge leads to better-served clients, a more fulfilling career as a true advisor, and a life more closely aligned with your values. By walking across this bridge, you can deliver your career to a place of authentic meaning—for your clients and for yourself. That place is difficult if not impossible to see, but it's there.

The bridge that takes you there has been rendered invisible—obscured by the constant pressure to develop your business by growing your client list rather than by servicing your ideal clients better. For decades, financial advisors and other professionals in advisory roles were told by their leadership, their partners, even themselves, to fatten their book of business. A beefier Rolodex, it was preached, was the way to a bigger piece of the pie. Sooner or later, the flaws in that mindset were evident to everyone who adopted it.

A more enlightened wing of the advisory business has long espoused a leaner book as the better way to grow. They cite the received wisdom of the 80/20 Rule, which in our business states that approximately 80 percent of your production will be derived from approximately 20 percent of your clients. The 80/20 Rule is no rule at all, but an immutable law of business physics. It's like denying gravity. We could flap our arms all day, but with the weight of our bloated books and collective denial, we were never going to fly.

So why has this essential business truth never fully penetrated the day-to-day management of our business?

There has been no bridge. Or, more accurately, the bridge was there all along, just unseen. In other words, there has been no process or business model that advisors can implement to transform the 80/20 Rule from a self-limiting clench to a liberating, income-multiplying force.

When Clients Attack

This was the situation we faced at Merrill Lynch: Our Financial Advisors (FAs) and our Client Associates (CAs) were drowning in their own success.

The bull market of the mid-1990s had brought in so many clients, so much business, and so much money that it was impossible to keep up with the demands. Bright, talented people were overwhelmed and exhausted. Some employees were leaving, downsizing to smaller firms, or retiring early. Even worse were the people who stayed and tried, heroically or foolishly, to keep up with the markets, the calls, and the crisis of the hour. That was success, yet it wasn't succeeding.

We tried to respond the way most panicked managers would, by hiring more people, specifically more CAs. But the Merrill senior leadership, and specifically our new Chief Executive Officer, Stan O'Neal, said no. Intuitively, he knew that more staff and higher payrolls weren't the solution. His insistence that we solve this problem without more staff was a pivot point.

In the district I was leading, the wake-up call came in the form of client satisfaction surveys. Though our production was consistently near or at the top of the company, our clients told us another story: They were unhappy with how we handled their phone calls and their requests. Their criticisms were direct, detailed, and disheartening. (They also didn't like hearing from their advisor only when they had something to sell, but we will talk more about that later.)

When Clients Leave

We had another problem, too, that was equally as troubling and infinitely more costly. Many of the clients who were getting the best service we could offer said, "We're leaving anyway." Some of these clients were friends and had long, complicated histories with us. They weren't the kind of clients who were going to attack us on a service survey. Their disappointment with us was deeper than any survey could go, and besides, they didn't want to hurt us. They liked us, but knew they needed something more— something we seemed incapable of delivering. They wanted the holistic and more personalized service the independents were offering. We anxiously offered discounts to keep them, but it had nothing to do with price and everything to do with everything else.

These smaller (but by no means insignificant) firms were offering genuine planning. They were responding to the core problem that high-net-worth individuals had: no plan and/or no ongoing process to implement the plan. It was especially widespread in the bull market of the day. All this emerging wealth was essentially unguided by client-specific plans and unsupported by a team prepared to implement them. The firms that realized this and moved into the planning business were beginning to pick off our best clients. One by one, we heard "thanks for the gains, but we need more than a broker now."

And you know what? They did.

Two Emergencies, One Question

The service surveys had a relevance that we could not overwrite with exceptional production data. Poor client service was festering just below the surface of our so-called success. And that very success was vulnerable, as our most profitable clients were leaving us because we simply didn't have the planning skills they so clearly needed and deserved.

We needed to solve each of these problems, yet there was no off-the-shelf answer. So we began with a simple question.

What Do Clients Really Want?

Clearly, the answer wasn't simply portfolio gains. We were excelling there. And it's not like our departing clients were getting ignored. We called them a lot. We had migrated much of our business to a fee-based model, which was supposed to foster a different kind of relationship. However, we found that even if the FA stops living on the kinetic energy of monthly production goals, the relationship still needed an engine to keep moving forward. It needs a reason. It needs a soul.

The independents eating our lunch were also fee based, but they weren't selling on that alone. They were attracting clients because they understood well what we were just coming to: planning creates a platform that locates advisors and brokers underneath it. They knew that advisors don't become planners just because they stop charging commissions and start charging fees. And knocking out a few financial plan binders, no matter how impressively fat, was not real planning.

The meaning of a plan varies from client to client, and our departing clients all wanted their plans specifically formulated to meet their financial needs and personal situations. As the saying goes, "The company that owns the plan owns the client." So if we were going to keep those clients and give them what we all knew they needed, we had to reintroduce ourselves to them as a company truly transformed. Sure, we could start planning, but that only got us even with the independents. We needed a *plan* for the plan.

That was the soft spot in the independents' business model. Their great planning was followed by so-so implementation, or worse. From what we could see, the first few months of a relationship were golden, full of wonderful conversations and reassuring feelings. "Finally," the clients would say, "We know where all this wealth is going." And then, the plan would sit there as the FA continued to attract more and more business from us (and other big firms). They didn't have a model for turning the plan into appropriate actions, and even if they had a model, they didn't have the time. The 80/20 Rule again. Here's where the story gets good, because we were onto something big, the second piece in the transformation.

Scheduled Contact: The Silver Bullet in Planning

Contact—meaningful, consultative, and scheduled. In Chapter 2, you'll see how we got there, and in Chapter 5, you'll see the full dimension of what we talk about when we talk to clients. Right now, the key take-away is this: When clients have regular, non-pressured, meaningful contact, they will rank their satisfaction higher.

That's intuitive, yet what surprised us was that contact out-ranked even investment performance as a measure of client satisfaction. Performance, it seemed, was the price of entry in the market. "I don't expect you to lose my money. I do expect something more," our clients were saying as they knocked our service or simply walked quietly to the door.

But if regular contact, meaningful plans, and consistent plan implementation were the antidotes, where in this world could our FAs and CAs find time in their chronically time-impoverished days? As it turns out, the answer wasn't in this world at all.

The Science of a Supernova

Supernovas are rare and spectacular. They occur when a so-called massive star, one at least eight times larger than our sun, has exhausted the nuclear fuel at its core, and the mass of the sur-rounding material is no longer sustainable. The star contracts, explosively, to a much smaller size, and in doing so creates another kind of celestial body that is both brighter and hotter than the original star.

The analogy is beautiful: an unsustainable mass, a dramatic and sudden contraction, and, consequently, a brighter burning light.

It's also what a group of remarkable people conceived and implemented at Merrill Lynch in the last years of the pre-vious century, and the first years of this one. Supernova, as it simply came to be known, was and is the process our advisory teams needed to elegantly live the 80/20 Rule, instead of being abused by it. Supernova led them out of unsustainable, unsatis-fying practices and into a new universe of loyal clients, reward-ing days, and higher revenue. With this book, you're invited to follow their path.

Where It Leads

But before we journey down that path, let's get back to the story: When Indiana Jones overcame his fears and stepped onto the invisible bridge, he wasn't at the end of the story. He still had a choice to make.

With his father's life slipping further away by the minute, a drink from the grail was the only way to save him. Arriving in the room where the grail is displayed, he found not one grail but many—false grails intended to confuse and distract. These grails were guarded by a knight of the First Crusade, sustained for over 700 years on the grail's power, an old warrior whose eyes are still shining brightly with secrets. Seeing quickly that he is no match for Indy's physical strength, he is about to speak to him when the two Nazi archaeologists who had followed Indy burst into the chamber. They gasp in amazement at the spectacular assortment of grails, as if each one had some of the true grail's power.

The old knight, who has seen others try and fail, knows that the grails' jewels and gold hypnotize with their proximity. As the Holy Grail holds great power, there are deadly consequences for those journeyers who mistakenly choose the incorrect grail. In a voice that carries both warning and promise, he says simply . . .

"Choose Wisely"

This was our message as we took Supernova across the country to Merrill Lynch districts. We weren't told to go by corporate leadership. District Directors took a leap of faith of their own and invited us. We heard: "My FAs are going to revolt if you don't bring that Supernova thing in here and train them." The word was spreading. There was a model of professional practice that let you be a true advisor—that helped you grow your business without destroying your life. Supernova was becoming a grail unto itself—nowhere close to holy, but compelling enough to send many FAs on a journey to find it.

Others found it, too. Supernova caught the attention of the business press and the upper echelons of business study. Our work was written up in *Fast Company*. *Registered Rep* magazine did a feature on Supernova. *Harvard Business Review* did a case study,[1] and the Massachusetts Institute of Technology (MIT) sent a team of grad students to study it.[2] Both the Harvard study and the MIT dissertation arrived at the same conclusion: Supernova worked. FAs were better advisors, clients were better served, and practices grew. All while in the powerful claws of a bear . . .

The Bear Was Back

The introduction of Supernova coincided with the burst bubbles of technology and telecom stocks, which dragged equities into the bear market of the early 2000s. 9/11 was such a violation and created so much fear that the environment for many Merrill FAs was even more desperate than before. Not only did they have too many clients, now many of them were anxious, or worse. It was the bear market that finally convinced hundreds of FAs that the only way out was across that bridge.

The researchers of the Harvard case validated the wisdom in that choice. They concluded that the down market eliminated a lot of the noise that makes tracking service performance difficult and the results unreliable. They held that the bear market gave Supernova an *even better reason to be*. Think about it, in a declining market, what's going to differentiate an advisor? It's service. It's real planning based on well-understood life goals.

---

[1]Rogelio Oliva, Roger Hallowell, and Gabriel Bitran. *Merrill Lynch: Supernova* (Harvard School of Business, 2003), http://harvardbusinessonline.hbsp. harvard.edu/b01/en/common/item_detail.jhtml;jsessionid=VKDOTTKCKR KIKAKRGWDR5VQBKE0YIISW?id=604053&referral=8636&_requestid=24291.

[2]Bassim Halaby and Qunmei Li. *Introducing Fundamental Changes to a Service Delivery Model: Lessons from a Financial Advisory Organization* (Alfred P. Sloan School of Management, Massachusetts Institute of Technology, 2002), http://dspace.mit.edu/handle/1721.1/8507.

That's what our clients told us before the market tanked, and it's what they told us after.

Arriving at Your Moment to Choose

Let's wind up the projector one more time—back to the grail chamber. . . .

Not hearing the caution in the old knight's voice, the Nazi seizes the most bejeweled grail and drinks greedily. Bad choice. Instead of life eternal, he got a wicked case of old age, going from about 50 to 500 in 6.2 seconds. The old knight wryly observes that he "did not choose wisely." Now, it's Indy's turn.

Indiana Jones understands intuitively that a carpenter would not possess a gaudy, decorative grail, so he chooses the most modest of the collection. A quick drink and a relieved moment later he is alive and off to save his father. For the Merrill Lynch advisors—the ones whose careers were faltering, whose marriages were suffering, whose ambitions to make a difference while making money were dying a little more with every insane day—the time was right. "Choose wisely," we said. Many did, and this book is what they have taught us.

They crossed the bridge and leaped into a new way of work, and wealth, and life. Their journey continues and now yours begins.

A Revolution from the Middle

Supernova was charged with electricity that was strong enough to jolt the entire Merrill Lynch organization. It was inspired action taken by the FAs in the vast middle of the company, and without really knowing it, we were part of a revolution in American business. We were leading from the middle.

Several authors have identified and explored the full dimension of this revolution. You can read:

- *Leading Quietly: An Unorthodox Guide to Doing the Right Thing* by Harvard's Joseph Badaracco (Harvard Business School Publishing, 2002).

- *Tempered Radicals* by Debra Meyerson (Harvard Business School Publishing, 2003).
- *Megatrends 2010* by Patricia Aburdene's (Hampton Roads Publishing Company, 2005); the shift in corporate leadership is described as if she were there for ours.

Supernova swept through Merrill Lynch powered by our peers. Senior leadership didn't mandate it. Training didn't teach it. We didn't put out a memo or make a slick video. We did, however, use a forum with a long and colorful history of inspiring cultural change. We staged a rock concert.

Hearing the Chants

Our team had made enough noise and drawn enough attention by what we had accomplished with our own Supernova experiment that other districts booked us for introduction meetings. The first few were just that—meetings. Been there. This deserved something bigger, and louder.

So the idea of a different kind of event began to gel, and then evolve, from New York City to Seattle. We put together a lineup of speakers, featuring the early Supernova superstars.

We also insisted on having every FA bring their CA. The CAs drive the effectiveness of a Supernova practice; they were the ones enduring the consequences of a bloated book so they needed to be in the room. Non-negotiable. In fact, we designed the entire experience right down to the music and, yes, the movie clip: You guessed it—Indiana Jones stepping onto the invisible bridge and choosing the true grail.

We arrived in the district for a day session and dinner with the leadership, the District Director, and all the managers. We trained them for a day, answered their questions, responded to their inquiries, and challenged their perceptions. Lively sessions all, and all essential to getting buy-in. We insisted on having the District Director on stage with us, so he or she had better be on board as well.

Then it was show time.

Helloooo, Detroit!

We weren't rock stars, but indulge me for a minute. Because I want you to know how remarkable it felt to be on that stage—in Dallas, or in New York at the Waldorf, or in Detroit, or in Los Angeles—with several hundred charged up advisors and their staffs responding to us, cheering for us, thanking us for giving them this amazing gift of Supernova.

It was equal parts church revival and Woodstock. People were testifying. People were saved. There were tears and bear hugs and smiles so big that we could see them through the stage lights.

Some of the best moments in my career happened at those events—on stage, with the FAs afterward, with my own team as we went through each of the evaluations right after we cleared the room. None of us took an early flight home so that everyone could gather to discuss the event and tighten our show. It never got old, and we never "mailed it in." You wouldn't have known that we actually had no intention of even doing a second event.

It's Yours—Go Do It; Go Coach It

Our original intent was to teach the Boston District how to implement Supernova and then let the Boston District teach the next district that asked, then that district teach the next, and so on. Didn't happen, and that's probably for the best. Supernova evangelism wasn't born overnight. A new district wasn't ready to lead another until they had fully inhabited the model and found their own voice, their own stars.

Yet, even then, the calls were coming in. We were asked by countless FAs to come teach it to them. Our response was the same: "Talk to your Director." We weren't going to storm into a district without the support of the District Director, and the District Director wasn't going to ask until he was so inundated with requests that he had no choice. You've seen the bumper sticker: "When the people lead, the leaders will follow."

So, like the performers who can't bear to disappoint their fans, we went out again and again. Over the course of two years, we introduced the Supernova service model to nearly every U.S. district in the Merrill Lynch organization. We were never told to go, and we were never told to stop. It was an undeniably powerful idea that arrived at precisely the right time.

All of this is remembered here to both honor the people who made Supernova happen and to help you understand its origins. Your own revolution can begin without the music and the spotlights. And if you do it right, people are still going to cheer.

The Steps on This Bridge

This book is about seeking the ultimate client experience and creating a rewarding new way to work by providing exceptional financial advice and service. Indiana Jones had his father's diary to guide him on his journey, complete with detailed drawings of supernatural icons and rubbings of writings found in ancient map rooms. You have this book, light on the supernatural but full of maps nonetheless, to guide you as you step onto the invisible bridge and implement Supernova.

You just read about Supernova's origins and the circumstances that practically willed it into being. In the first chapter, you'll see what happened when the 80/20 Rule asserted itself with a vengeance, and seemed to create nothing but walls all around us. In the second chapter, you'll see how we began to find our footing out, through a client contact system we called 12/4/2. In Chapters 3 through 7, you'll take the very specific steps along the invisible bridge that will deliver you and your team to the goal of becoming a Supernova Advisor.

Scattered throughout the book are sidebars filled with ideas and parallel thoughts that didn't fit neatly into the text, but are essential nevertheless.

You'll also get a brace of reality in the form of Failure Points Analysis. As with any journey, you are bound to encounter roadblocks that might deter you from reaching your ideal destination. The same is true for Supernova. Throughout Chapters 3 through 7, I've identified the most common reasons why Supernova fails, and what to be vigilant of as you work to make it succeed.

In the key chapters, you'll be delivered to your own moments of truth. These are exercises and challenges at the chapters' ends called "Leaps." Take them. They will enrich your experience and accelerate your journey.

Now, it's time to take that first step on the invisible bridge. . . .

CHAPTER 1

The Trouble with Success

THE TYRANNY OF THE 80/20 RULE

In This Chapter

- The 80/20 Rule is historically relevant and uncannily accurate across industries and generations.
- In financial services, the 80/20 Rule states that approximately 80 percent of your production is derived from approximately 20 percent of your clients. This is an essential understanding and the foundation for Supernova.

There are five stars in the Supernova practice model. They all are contained within the steadfast application of the 80/20 Rule.

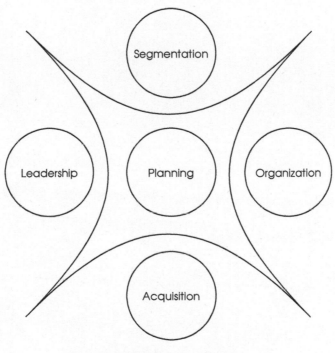

The Five Principles of Supernova

Merrill Lynch Financial Advisor Jim McEnerney was on a binge again. It was before Supernova, and once again, he was having a difficult time saying no to his many clients.

New clients were coming in the door and Jim was holding it open. As he confidently shook their hand, took their money, and then tried, once again, to manage the relationship, you could almost hear him thinking, "I can handle it this time." His confidence was the outgrowth of the past year or so, which had been relatively satisfying—relative, at least, to the year before that. During *that* period, Jim and his team had lost control of their business. Whether they were ready to admit it or not, they were starting to lose control all over again.

Financial advisors (FAs), like Jim, are organized in entrepreneurial groups. These are free-standing businesses with their own strategies, processes, and profits and losses (P&Ls). It's a common structure within the major brokerage and advisory firms. When these groups are working well, they are beautiful businesses to observe, coach, and learn from. When they are dysfunctional, or failing outright, there's still plenty to learn.

This vicious cycle once again seizing Jim was spinning wildly throughout Merrill. There were groups that grasped the intuitive power of the 80/20 Rule and made various attempts to obey it. They ran the gamut from ineffectual to ham-fisted, but they all shared one particular failure: It never lasted. Every time they trimmed their book of business, it was only a matter of time before saying "no" became impossible once again. It was "yes, yes, and yes" to more clients in an accelerating cycle. They were bingeing again on new business, and like all binges past a certain point, it was getting ugly.

Jim recalls, "It wasn't about staffing; it was about process. We simply didn't have a way to manage our clients, so, naturally, they were managing us—and clients, God bless them, are ruthless managers."

"I wasn't productive. I was dealing with the urgent, but not the important. When I look back on those days, I'm amazed at how far away I was from what I value most. It was unsustainable as a business, but beyond that, it was just wrong."

Unsustainable and just plain wrong. It was also predicted to happen, with precision, well over 100 years ago.

Pareto's Discovery and the Beginning of the Vital Few

The underlying pattern that supports the 80/20 Rule was discovered in 1897 by Vilfredo Pareto, an Italian economist examining patterns of wealth and income in nineteenth-century England. Not surprising then (or now) his research proved that roughly 80 percent of England's wealth was possessed by 20 percent of the people. Yet, his real surprise came in the discovery of a consistent mathematical relationship between the percentage of the population and the percentage of wealth they possessed. He found that this correlation persisted in England, and throughout Europe, in his time and in previous eras. He could demonstrate with relative precision that there was a predictable *imbalance* exerting itself. From that moment on, a series of big thinkers—including the people you'll meet in this book—would put that force to work.

In 1949, Harvard professor George Zipf called the 80/20 Rule the Principle of Least Effort. Building on Parareto's theory of imbalance, he lectured that 20 to 30 percent of productive resources (people, time, skills, etc.) will consistently account for 70 to 80 percent of the activity related to that resource. Again, he discussed the predicable imbalance that exists, which is counterintuitive to the more common democratic expectation that all clients are equal or that every day has roughly the same significance. Call this the 50/50 Fallacy, because it rarely is fact.

The first guru of the Quality Movement, Joseph Moses Juran alternately called the 80/20 Rule the Pareto Principle or the Rule of the Vital Few. Using the key concepts of this principle, he sought to uncover quality failures and improve reliability. Japanese automobile companies were the first to turn his ideas into business processes. Juran even took up residence in Japan and then returned to the United States. In the States, domestic manufacturers clamored to learn what Japan had mastered: 80 percent of the errors can be traced to 20 percent of the activities. Fix that 20 percent and the cars get better in a hurry.

Even when one suspects there is an imbalance affecting results, the actual numbers tend to exceed our estimation, if not shock us outright. Seeing the documented imbalance in, say, revenue across the business, can freeze us with indecision. Acting on the imbalance means making radical changes, and most people would probably do what Jim McEnerney did—just snap on his blinders and keep plowing.

Because the Money Kept Coming

It was happening at Merrill, just like it happens in nearly every consultative company. There was a culture that rewarded customer accumulation over customer service. It's not that customer service was ignored or considered irrelevant. In fact, the company regularly measured client service and made that information available to every FA. One of the most significant changes in Merrill's business model had made the company more service focused: the migration to annuitized relationships, not merely transactional ones.

As more and more groups within Merrill tied their revenue to their clients' portfolio performance versus what they could sell that month, client service "improved." I add the quotations marks here because, all too often, the so-called improvement was merely a change in how often an FA contacted a client—instead of calling with a pitch, the FA just didn't call. To many customers, that was indeed an improvement, even if they weren't getting better service.

Despite the annuitized model, the accumulation culture was still alive and well. Gathering assets was where the money was. Teams and FAs were recognized and rewarded for growing their assets under management. Poor service scores were just a sign that the team needed to hire more help for the phones, serve clients better coffee, or something else. No one knew that quality service meant more.

Moreover, incentives to deliver better service weren't part of the picture. The response to poor service score was never punitive. The response to high production was always positive. And during the go-go days of the late 1990s and into 2000, there was plenty of production to reward. Who cared if 20 percent of your clients were generating 80 percent or more of your revenue? The goal was to earn more revenue, not to overthink where it came from. But when that revenue stopped coming, the 80/20 Rule began to matter very much.

But before you move on, let's hear the rest of Jim McEnerney's story. It's where you're heading if you can implement Supernova as well as Jim and his team did. Jim says:

> After we stopped kidding ourselves about where our business was really coming from versus where our time was going, we segmented our book using Supernova. It was a wrenching few weeks, but worth it. I'm a nicer person to be around, believe me.
>
> They don't know the name, but my clients are well aware of how we used the process to reduce our client list down to our very best. They're proud of it actually. We know it's sunk in when they ask us in a meeting if we are accepting new clients.

Final word: Supernova segmentation is *not* about merely reducing your book. It's about giving your clients exceptional service. And the only way to do that is to know who they are.

CHAPTER 2

Contact

THE HUMBLE FOUNDATION OF THE ULTIMATE CLIENT EXPERIENCE

In This Chapter

- Fee-based models of revenue do not lead directly to exceptional client service.
- Exceptional service is a perception; it's harder to measure than portfolio value and differs from one client to the next.
- In our investigation, exceptional service has five distinct components, with "Scheduled contact and meaningful conversations" as the primary driver.
- The Supernova contact ritual: 12/4/2. Twelve scheduled contacts (one a month), 4 of the 12 include quarterly reviews of the full portfolio, 2 of the scheduled reviews are face-to-face meetings with a broad agenda. 12/4/2.
- Discipline is a drain on energy. Rituals keep energy free for better purposes. Supernova client contact is a ritual, not a discipline.

The story of how Supernova formed a bridge to exceptional service picks up just as Merrill's private client group was becoming a better organization. As mentioned in Chapter 1, Financial Advisors (FAs) were migrating to an annuitized or fee-based business model. More and more FAs were beginning to make their money on management fees tied to percentages of the portfolio value, not commissions tied to trades or transactions. It's what clients told us they wanted, and it makes perfect sense. The table was set perfectly for FAs to become true advisors, instead of salespeople.

But there was a problem—with no sales calls to make, there was no reason to call clients at all. In their case study of Supernova, the authors at the Harvard School of Business called this temptation to coast "the golf problem." Said one FA in the case study: "The soft underbelly of annuitized business is that unless you commit to providing a certain level of service, once you're being paid whether or not you do anything, there is less incentive to contact your client. Supernova solves that problem."[1]

But, before Supernova could solve this problem, we first had to diagnose it.

[1]Rogelio Oliva, Roger Hallowell, and Gabriel Bitran. *Merrill Lynch: Supernova* (Harvard School of Business, 2003), http://harvardbusinessonline.hbsp .harvard.edu/b01/en/common/item_detail.jhtml;jsessionid=VKDOT TKCKRKIKAKRGWDR5VQBKE0YIISW?id=604053&referral=8636&_ requestid=24291.

Our district was leading, or finishing second in nearly every category that measured production—both client acquisition and asset growth—yet we were finishing at or near the bottom in service rankings. This paradoxical evaluation was stubborn and confounding. Poor client service persisted no matter how much asset growth or money under management we acquired. In fact, all that money coming in was aggravating an already festering issue. It was getting worse over time, not better. We were missing something important. Receiving poor service scores was like throwing a bucket of ice water on the hot, hard-revving engine of our district's performance. Yet if performance wasn't what clients wanted from us, what was?

"Talk to Me—Here's When"

Jim Walker, the sales manager for the district, and I embarked on a journey to discover what clients craved most. During this exploration, we talked to our clients and to the few FAs in our region who stood out among our uniformly poor client service scores. We consulted the business literature and visited various business schools. We inhabited the question of what client's want from us as fully as we possibly could. We learned that the importance that our clients placed on growing their portfolio value wasn't even in the top five. Here's what Jim said:

> Good service is a perception . . . where profit and loss are easy to measure and rank, feelings are moving targets. We discovered that to succeed in the realm of perception, the essential mechanism is regular, scheduled contact. Once we absorbed that simple fact, Supernova began to form.

What Drives Exceptional Service

From our discovery process, we concluded that there are five important drivers of exceptional service. The list begins with the core insight that we build Supernova around, they are:

1. *Scheduled contacts and conversations.* Clients want personal-ized, nonpressurized, high-quality contact; *and* they want to have it on their calendar, not just find us on the other end of an unexpected call.
2. *Rapid response to problems.* Intuitively, we knew this, yet with an unmanageably large group of clients, FAs and their teams were continually reacting.
3. *Attention to details.* Again, intuitive, but impossible to suc-ceed with an overloaded mind.
4. *Anticipating issues before they become urgent.* Anticipation is the opposite of reaction. We were reacting and not much else.
5. *Depth and breadth of services offered.* A corporate advantage at Merrill, but were we leveraging it? Hardly.

The power in that list begins and ends with number one; that is, exceptional client service depends on high-quality, scheduled client contact. Personal time together is important to the health of any good relationship. Conversation deepens your mutual understanding. And there's something about being around a table that leads to good conversation, as anyone who has lingered around the dinner table can attest. Meetings also give clients an opportunity to experience the FA's professional-ism in a manner that phone calls simply can't.

The implications of this insight were enormous.

Doing the Math on Client Contact

The current fee-based business model practiced at Merrill had no regularly scheduled contact built in. If anything, it was just the opposite: irregular contact that was typically in response to a client issue—a request, question, or problem. If consistent contact that provides value is the number one driver of client service, and the current best practices had nothing of the sort, then the first order of business was clear.

Working with the clarity that comes from a true insight, we began the next investigation: How regularly should the contact occur? And what are we going to talk about?

High-net-worth individuals (like just about everyone) value their time as much as their money. They'll spend an hour on a call or in a meeting if they believe it's important. They might even enjoy themselves. But veer into the irrelevant or into inane sales chat, and you're creating ill will that sets the relationship back. As such, the first rule of high-quality, scheduled contact was to stay focused and stay relevant. And what's the most relevant communication that investors receive from their banks or money managers? The statement.

Statements arrive monthly and quarterly. After some experimentation with groups in our region, that frequency was proving to be effective. It also provided us with a framework for relevant client communication and advisor contact. Think about it: FAs and clients could engage in monthly contact to answer questions and get answers when the statement arrived. Then, when the four quarterly statements arrived, they could engage in more in-depth sessions that would also include quarterly reviews of the full relationship. Two of those quarterly reviews would be on the phone, and two would be in person. Now do the math: 12 monthly statements, 4 quarterly reviews, and 2 face-to-face meetings, which all together add up to the 12/4/2 ritual.

Why twice a year? Simply put, once is not enough, and we'd be intruding too much in a client's life and infringing on their schedule if we tried to make each of the quarterly reviews in person.

The Supernova Contact Ritual: 12/4/2

12/4/2: 12 scheduled contacts (one a month), 4 of which include quarterly reviews of the full portfolio, with 2 of the scheduled quarterly reviews as 60 minute face-to-face meetings with a broad agenda. 12/4/2.

In Chapter 4, you'll see what it looks like down to the minute. But let's stay with the big picture a little longer.

Our investigation indicated that client satisfaction was connected to regular and scheduled contact that added value, not sales hassle. 12/4/2 addresses this need with a regimented, value-rich contact process. So, one would think that once we implemented 12/4/2, our client service scores should take off like a rocket, right?

Hardly. 12/4/2 also has an unseen asterisk floating above it. We saw it, our FAs saw it, and you can probably see it, too. Because in the environment in which it was conceived—late in the bull market of the 1990s and in the emergency rooms of our FAs—implementing 12/4/2 was impossible. Not only aren't there enough hours in the day to provide regular contact to numerous clients (although after implementing Supernova, there are more than enough); there wasn't a process for anyone to commit to. And even if there were, would anyone have the discipline?

Contact Is Not <u>Discipline—It's Ritual</u>

In their fantastic book *The Power of Full Engagement* (Simon & Schuster, 2003), Jim Loehr and Tony Schwartz present an idea central to their startlingly potent premise that "managing energy, not time, is the key to high performance and personal renewal." They maintain that personal discipline is overrated as a factor in success. The authors use tennis great Ivan Lendl as a central example, focusing on his extraordinary series of mental rituals that kept him centered and focused. They say:

> It is perfectly logical to assume that Lendl excelled in part because he had extraordinary will and discipline. That probably isn't so. A growing body of research suggests that as little as 5 percent of our behaviors are consciously self-directed. We are creatures of habit and as much as 95 percent of what we do occurs automatically or in reaction to a demand or an anxiety. What Lendl understood brilliantly and instinctively was the power of positive rituals—precise, consciously acquired behaviors that become automatic in our lives, fueled by a deep sense of purpose. (p. 166)

There's more I want to show you from the book because it presents the most effective system for personal and professional growth that I have ever seen. For years, I've taken teams to Jim Loehr's clinics on his Corporate Athlete Training System, and the principle of ritual versus discipline is a touchstone that I return to again and again. Again, from the book:

> It is easy to dismiss as rigid and even extreme the highly structured routines of an athlete like Ivan Lendl. But stop for a moment and think about the people you admire—or simply look at the areas in your life in which you are most effective and productive. If you are like most of our clients, you already have many rituals in place—often outside your conscious awareness. These may range from habits of hygiene to planning the day ahead to routines with your family. Far from precluding spontaneity, these rituals provide a level of comfort, continuity, and security that frees us to improvise and to take risks. . . . *Rituals provide a stable framework in which creative breakthroughs often occur.* (p. 168)

I have emphasized the last line because I believe that the impact of that idea on our professional lives is significant. In fact, it's what makes 12/4/2 work. FAs couldn't will their practices to change anymore than they could will the bond market to change. They could, however, implement positive rituals that create opportunities for true game-changing insights to emerge. After all, will power demands power, and power is a surprisingly limited resource. Use it wisely. From the book once more:

> Since will and discipline are far more limited and precious resources than most of us realize, they must be called upon very selectively. Because even small acts of self-control use up this limited reservoir, consciously using this energy for one activity means it will be less available for the next one. The sobering truth is that we have the capacity for very few conscious acts of self-control in a day. (p. 169)

Let's Refocus

This was the situation: Business was great because, well, business was great. The markets were up. The economy was creating jobs. The new economy was creating exuberant glee—irrational to be sure, but certainly an amazing time to be in the financial advisory business. Internet trading and self-directed portfolios were succeeding because hot stocks were easy to pick. Investing had become America's number one spectator sport, and our FAs had been on the field a long, long time.

The service scores were the wake-up call, and our investigation into alternative approaches came just ahead of the bursting of the Internet bubble. Bad stock performance brought good companies down, and portfolios that had been multiplying were suddenly and viciously contracting. Think client calls were tough to manage in good times? Try taking them all after the impact of losses fully registered. Oh, and there's a new marketing focus this quarter. Get busy.

At this point, our FA teams were about ready to jump off a cliff. We had something there to support them when they did; they just couldn't see it yet.

CHAPTER

Segmentation

THE SUPERNOVA NON-NEGOTIABLE

In This Chapter

- Supernova is impossible without a manageable client list. One hundred clients is the optimal number.
- Production-per-client shapes what your segmented book looks like, but it's not the only factor.
- Growth of assets under management is a product of a well-implemented Supernova. If fewer clients meant less growth, there would be no reason to implement it.
- Min/max is critical. Set a minimum threshold of assets per client along with your maximum number of clients. The growth is in continually moving your minimum upward.
- Segmentation is about maintaining high standards and helping every client get the exceptional service they deserve.
- Communication is vital. Talk to your clients on both sides of the segmentation divide about the reasons why.

Segmentation is the first step in the Supernova journey. For some, it's the most difficult. For all, it's essential.

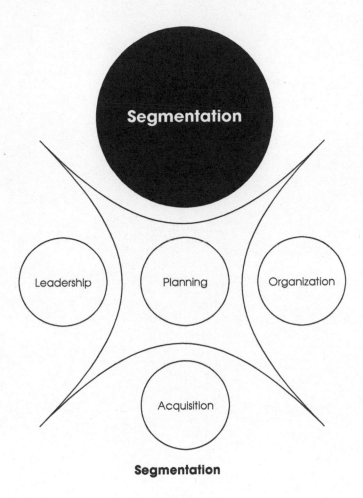

Segmentation

Your introduction is complete. You've seen the environment that made Supernova necessary. You've learned about the 12/4/2 contact ritual that gives it its underlying vitality. You've been shown our earned wisdom on how client contact forms the foundation of exceptional customer experience. Now it's time to get serious. Now it's time to segment.

Without segmentation, there is no Supernova. Understanding this in its fullest implications, and then acting on it decisively, is what ignites Supernova.

Segmentation of an unmanageable client load is not a best practice worth observing and adapting. It's not a suggestion or a recommendation. It is an absolute. There is no other way to implement Supernova—no other way to succeed *unless* you can deliver exceptional service and then transform your client's inevitable satisfaction into growth.

Segmentation is the point at which faith in the invisible bridge will be tested most acutely. You must believe it in order to take that first cautious step. But in the primordial days of early Supernova, it was more like walking the plank.

"You're on Service Probation"

There actually was no such thing as service probation, but the five financial advisors (FAs) at risk of getting shown the door at Merrill didn't know that. They *did* know that their service scores were horrible and that their production was hampered by the nonstop emergency room they were running for their clients. These FAs were all failing. We needed a laboratory to test our hunches on contact and especially on segmentation—hence, service probation.

We told them what they already knew: what they were doing was not working. Then we told them that they had two options: "Try this new way of working or try another profession." The full mandate to these FAs was:

> You need a completely different business model. With this one, you're going to deliver exceptional service. You're going to have 12 scheduled contacts a year. You're going to give them four comprehensive reviews, with two of them in person. You're going to respond rapidly to their questions and problems. You will create a financial plan for every client and you will implement that plan. Sounds like a lot of work, right? It is. But it's possible because you will have only 100 clients, and those clients will be the referral engine that drives your business growth.

Trusting souls that they were, they agreed. Not that they had much of a choice.

In truth, no FA really has much choice if they intend to deliver the service promises that they make to high-net-worth clients. Still, we could not have foreseen what game-changing moments these were. Who would have guessed that within a half a year, we would be standing on stages in hotel ballrooms from coast to coast, holding Supernova kickoff sessions that rivaled tent revivals with their energy and enthusiasm. Supernova, with all of its peer-to-peer momentum, was about to explode on the Merrill Lynch landscape. Yet, when we told these FAs to segment down or pack it up, we didn't even have a name for the model.

The First Hurdles

After informing the five FAs of the new game plan, we told them to go home, reintroduce themselves to their spouses and their kids and to identify their 100 best clients using production and assets as the criteria. (Later in this chapter, we'll get to the rationale for 100, and learn about other, more nuanced, processes for screening clients.) We told them we'd handle the business of telling their clients that another FA team was going to advise them from now on—and do a better job of it. It turns out those were easy calls to make; most of the clients were unhappy anyway. Remember, those low services scores came from somewhere.

As our experiment began, we quickly identified a need. The FAs needed a spreadsheet calendar that listed every scheduled client call for the month ahead. Every day was planned down to the hour, with enough flexibility to accommodate unplanned issues and new business efforts. Our contact management package at the time, ACT!, was vertical. We needed something horizontal, so we created a spreadsheet in Excel that looked across the entire month. That gave their days and their months a highly visible path to follow, and follow they did.

In addition to watching their adherence to the 12/4/2 contact ritual, we also began measuring their service scores with weekly surveys of the clients they had been in contact with. And every week, we got more and more juiced by the ascending scores. We were witnessing what exceptional service looked like and the organizational structure required to support it. It was during this time that we even named this phenomenon.

Failure Points Analysis

Five Reasons Why Supernova Fails

Supernova is no miracle cure. It requires significant initial change and sustained commitment. It's work. It's also invigorating and profitable. Yet, most FAs don't realize Supernova's true power. Some get close, then slip back into old patterns. Others fail completely. Why? Look at the list below. As mentioned in the Introduction, we're going to identify these roadblocks into the relevant failure points throughout the remaining chapters

(Continued)

and suggest ways in which they can be overcome. So be on the lookout for Failure Points Analyses or see if you can anticipate them.

1. No segmentation.
2. Never turning the schedule over to the client associate (CA).
3. Poor adherence to 12/4/2 and to scheduled days.
4. Failure to use available time for growth.
5. Poor accountability.

It's important to mention that not every FA involved in the experiment succeeded. Of the five, two FAs turned it into gold and growth. One FA compromised his early success by failing to hold his clients to 100. The other two FAs simply could not stay organized in the 12/4/2 process and eventually resigned. Knowing what we know today about how to coach the model, I think we'd keep at least four of these five FAs performing at high levels, but at that time we had seen enough to know that it worked.

In fact, one of the winning FAs actually named this business structure. With his voice literally full of awe, he said that this thing was "like a supernova." A what? He explained that this business practice was like a star that contracts to its thermonuclear core and then expands to become a hotter, brighter, larger star. "Cool," we thought, "we'll call it Supernova."

Segmentation 101 to 401

We've learned a lot about segmentation over the years. It can be as simple as identifying your ideal clients based on the dollars they mean to you, or it can be a wholly individualized and detailed examination of not only where the money comes from but also where the potential for more lies. The latter approach was undertaken by George Kempf, another one of the first Supernova adopters. George, however, began to implement Supernova on his own without a threat of probation, real or otherwise.

George came to Merrill as a third career, after being a trader and a corporate marketer. He says, "What was missing was a sense of meaning—I wanted to help people succeed, not just companies," says George, and a career as an FA seemed to fit the bill perfectly. He joined the company, relocated his family, and began building a book of business by focusing on creating financial plans for his clients. We called them Financial Foundations. They were a comparative rarity in the early 1990s. Not for George, though.

By 1997 George had gathered $48 million dollars in assets, and generated $442,000 in production in one year alone. He had 631 accounts and completed 211 Financial Foundations, but he was one miserable FA. Here's what George said:

> I was using planning as leverage to get business but had become far too busy to do any real planning. More business was not helping me help anybody, but I was trapped—both by my thinking and by a culture of growth over all else. I was overwhelmed and exhausted.

Segmentation Isn't Subtle

You've probably already experimented with segmentation without genuinely segmenting. Many advisors have gone into their book and identified their ideal clients, their second best clients, the clients they tolerate, and the clients they'd like to hand off but haven't gotten around to it. Sound familiar? You might have even begun to change how you interact with each group. The problem is that these segmentation systems are all shaded gray; that is, the difference between clients is less distinct and vulnerable to changes day to day. Besides, your CA doesn't have the time to decode the subtle differences between these categorized clients. When the phone rings, it's a client calling. Period. Good client, okay client, difficult client—they all have needs, and the CA needs to move them on, dragging your effectiveness along. If you segment like this, you have not segmented for Supernova.

George was also a Supernova pioneer. He was one of the visionary FAs who helped demonstrate to the entire organization that there was, in fact, an invisible bridge across the canyon of crazy-making behavior. He took the leap of faith—he segmented. Then we eagerly watched what happened. The truth is that we weren't quite sure it was going to work, because George didn't just segment or cut down his book, he eviscerated it— from over 600 clients to just 33.

We'll return to the segmentation process George conceived and executed later in this chapter. Before we do, a clarification. Supernova segmentation isn't about working less or avoiding the stress of high performance.

Supernova demands your best work, in part, because a successful Supernova practice is constantly growing.

Growth is why you segment, and segmenting is the only way to grow. Of course, that proof is more evident now than it was then to Tony Singh.

Tony Singh and the Thousand-Yard Stare

Tony is a Merrill Lynch FA with a remarkable story that includes chapters as a pilot in the Pakistani air force, a cab driver in the United States, and a wildly successful FA for Merrill. He's an entire book unto himself and very helpful for this one. As one of the first FAs to adopt Supernova, Tony ensured that the first two tenets of the model—segmentation and organization— were squarely focused on the third—acquisition. In other words, before he could make the leap of faith onto the invisible bridge, he also needed to believe that his business was going to step up—and step up in the right way. Tony stepped onto the invisible bridge with his eyes locked on growth.

> Supernova looks like it's making your job easier. It's not.
> It's changing where you work hard, and I adopted it only
> because I absolutely believed that my business could grow

larger by first making it smaller. Once I believed that—a belief based on what I saw with other early adopters, and in my own gut—I saw nothing else.

Today, Tony's business is a high-performance, highly profitable mechanism of steady, managed growth. Segmentation is about growth, not retreat. That doesn't mean it's easy. After all, it's never easy getting rid of a suit you've gotten used to, even if it doesn't fit perfectly anymore.

I Like Suits—Bet You Do, Too

Let's say you really like the process of buying suits—you love the atmosphere of a good haberdasher and all the small decisions that go into finding a great suit. Now think of buying suits as the process of acquiring and efficiently servicing new business. It's at once comfortable and exciting, and over the years you have developed a really big collection of suits. You keep buying suits, but your closet space stays the same—you have only enough room to keep 20 suits in good shape, unless you resort to cramming them into increasingly smaller and smaller spaces. Some of the less worn ones are practically wadded up in the corner. For a person who loves suits, you certainly are treating them shabbily.

Grief and the FA: A Love Story

It hurts to end a relationship, especially a long-term one, even when it's clearly not working. Endings cause grief. Our FAs expressed one or all of the well-known stages of grief: denial, anger, bargaining, and depression. Many of these clients were among the FAs first. They were intensely loyal to them, even if they were rarely in contact with them or knew little of their current situation. Yet, that lack of connection and communication is the real sadness. Don't they deserve better? What is best for them, minimal service from you or exceptional service from a

(Continued)

deeply committed FA who has included that client in his or her segmented practice? You know the answer. Love can mean letting go and accepting people as they truly are. Acceptance. That's the final stage of grief, and an optimal state of being when you are segmenting with Supernova.

Segmentation is about knowing exactly which suits fit you best right now, and giving away the rest of them to your friends and family members who also love suits. But, of course, you still like buying suits, and new ones are continually finding their way into your closet. That's who you are. But your closet space hasn't changed, and at the end of the year you once again must make hard decisions about which are your ideal suits and give away the rest of them to loving homes. Then, you will have 20 great suits that perfectly fit within your closet, and you're happy.

It was the same situation with our FAs—too many suits and too little closet space (still is with plenty, and is the industry norm in many sales and advisory-oriented industries). The typical FA might have 500 clients or more and simply can't give them good service—there isn't enough room in the closet or, more accurately, time in the day. What's more, most of these clients aren't even capable of being very profitable anymore.

Although the 80/20 principle is reasserting itself, how can you know which 20 percent of your clients are delivering 80 percent of your profit? Clients aren't suits; a real methodology is required. It's an analysis that can be automated and pretty simple, or it can be highly nuanced. Let's look at the latter and revisit George Kempf.

The 11 Screens

George didn't begin his Supernova segmentation with 33 clients as the goal. He thought 100 sounded about right. Five years of experience in coaching and learning from other FA teams tells me that 100 is about the right size, but we didn't know that then. So when George came to me in a state of near exhaustion, all we decided to do was thoroughly break down his book and see who was paying him.

The process he employed over the next four months is what he later called his 11 screens, which are both intuitive and instructive. Let's hear from George again:

> One hundred clients seemed about right, but could I make a living on that few? You don't know unless you analyze the business, and the first three reports my assistant and I generated were the obvious first steps. We began with standard Merrill reporting on (1) production by account, (2) assets by account, and (3) priority clients, which was an internal definition of either $250,000 in assets or $5,000 in annual production. It was an interesting exercise, and we we're surprised by how little overlap there was.
>
> For example, the production list told us I had received fee or commission revenue from 500 of our 631 accounts—131 of my accounts were essentially inactive. What's more, 90 percent of my production came from just 13 percent of my clients. I had clients with million-dollar balances and zero production—we were their checking account. And several low-asset clients generated significant production.
>
> With the three lists in front of us, we dug deeper. In addition to the inactive accounts, we found several more with very minimal production, and they had resisted whatever attempts we made to learn more. These weren't relationships, they were mere buyers.
>
> Still, we weren't a whole lot closer to knowing who our best 100 clients were.

What George did next is where Supernova segmentation begins to become as much art as it is science. He took his book through more subjective screens: Did he like the client and did the client like him? Did they believe in his managed-money approach, or were they just using him as a broker? Did they have the ability to implement his Financial Foundation plan? Could they realistically become a premier client?

Lots of questions and lots of lists, yet surprisingly little insight. No one screen delivered 100 clients, so he came up with another screening method by using more objective data: profit. George says:

> We were traveling to see several clients, and incurring hard costs. And we were incurring soft costs in the form of work-hours from me and my assistant. We got totals by account on hard-dollar and soft-dollar profitability. Then we added a price-value screen; we wanted to know who was demanding discounts and who believed the value of our service was worth the price.

George's final screen was potential—which clients through referral, networking assistance, or growth of their own business were the best bets to propel his future growth? Finally, after 4 months and 11 screens, the answer was clear—right, George?

> I was still baffled. We hadn't reached 100 clients on any screen, so we said, "What the heck—are there any clients who meet the criteria on all 11 screens?" You guessed it: There were only 33, which represented about 100 accounts. Then, as a joke really, we looked at the previous year's business and totaled the income I received from those 33 clients. That's when we were really floored. To give up 83 percent of our accounts, we gave away just 9 percent of our production, about $39,000. Both my assistant and I just stared at the numbers, thinking back on the year and how hard we worked, how many hours it took, all to generate less than 10 percent of our production.

That was an important "aha moment" for everyone watching the Supernova experiment. But a 33-relationship book seemed so counterintuitive, so opposed to the Merrill culture or any sales culture. We resisted. We reviewed his screens. In the end, the numbers were just too compelling. The 80/20 Principle—which in George's case was closer to 90/10—was asserting itself yet again. We obeyed it, and with George, we stepped onto the bridge.

George Kempf's 11 Screens

1. Account by production
2. Value of assets
3. Priority client status
4. Likeability
5. Approach buy-in
6. Financial wherewithal
7. Priority client capability
8. Hard-dollar profitability
9. Soft-dollar profitability
10. Price-value perception
11. Opportunity for future growth

Client Upgrades, Client Handoffs

For George and for every FA who had effectively segmented, two kinds of calls had to take place next. You might think that telling your clients that they essentially "made the cut" would be easy and only the "we're handing you off" calls would be tough. In reality, both represent a major change in the relationship dynamic. Change is inherently uncertain, and uncertainty equals anxiety. It's true in financial markets, and it's true in financial relationships.

So let's talk about how we framed the first task, certainly the more pleasant of the two, but not the easiest to talk about since there was no script. No team at Merrill (or anywhere else I knew of) had undergone such a radical transformation in observance of the 80/20 Rule. Remember the suit analogy? We used another one here. . . .

We said that we were creating an all-first-class airline and that the client was on the passenger list. It was a small plane, and everyone on board would be in first class. We said we were going to give the client first-class service for a year, and if that was too much for them and they preferred another kind of relationship, we'd be happy to do that. But here's what their first-class service would look like: There would be regular, scheduled contact. We described the nature of this contact by telling them when and what each meeting or call was going to entail. We told them about 12/4/2. We told them that by reducing our client roster, we were going to be able to commit the time to do for them what we promised at the first meeting. Simply put, we were going to be true advisors.

It was liberating, and it was just weird. But most clients got it. Some loved the idea. Some had a wait-and-see mind-set. Some were afraid that their presence on the new list was going to last only as long as it took to attract a client with more assets.

Once we began to fulfill our contact commitments, we started to hear this: "I get it, okay. So what you're doing is you're giving me a different kind of advisory experience than we had before. I understand first class and I certainly don't want to ride in coach."

"Wait, Wait! Don't Leave Me!"

Segmentation is a moment of truth for our clients as well. When some clients saw how serious our FAs were about delivering exceptional service, and offering it to only a limited number of clients, they offered to bring the rest of their assets under our management. We need to be clear—Supernova isn't about ultimatums and boxing your clients into choices they don't want to make. If your clients want a high level of service, and have the minimum assets you require and fit the screens you have established, welcome them to a new kind of financial advisory.

With a segmented book and the 12/4/2 contact ritual, we were finally in a position to create unique value every time we talked to our clients. There was no selling. There was only conversation. We finally had time to develop an authentic financial plan and time to put that plan into action.

We talked about taxes; we talked about estate planning; we talked about insurance, mortgages, or their business. We asked: What kind of values did they want to pass on? What were they passionate about? What was missing? Every contact was a conversation, and every conversation had a larger purpose of simplifying our client's lives and helping them leverage their wealth to create a more meaningful life. In essence, we became stewards of their wealth and their time. In its fullest expression, stewardship has measurable value to high-net-worth clients. They are smart people who don't want to make a dumb decision. Salespeople pushed them into dumb decisions. As true advisors, we don't and won't.

Our clients—all clients—deserve a true advisor working from a personalized plan. With Supernova segmentation, we were finally able to give it to them. The other good news is we didn't have to leave our other clients standing at the curb while we boarded all those first-class flights.

For the Rest: Good Advice in the Right Size

The initial implementation of Supernova intersected fortuitously with another Merrill service, the Merrill Lynch Financial Advisory Center, or FAC. This was a telephone-only service staffed with salaried, registered professionals who were both well trained and well supported. They knew how to provide effective service to smaller clients. They had software tools that helped them bring a great deal of continuity to each call, no matter which Merrill person was taking it.

The FAC was one option, and it worked very well for many clients who were relocated there. Anecdotes and hard data confirmed it. FAs heard back from clients who felt much better served, and service scores climbed for nearly all the clients who migrated to FAC.

Today, George's business has grown well past the 33 original Supernova relationships he began with. His story demonstrates that with the right kind of staffing and sharp organization (that's the next chapter) an FA can be a very effective advisor to about 100 clients. This brings us to important component in managing Supernova—staying segmented after you've segmented.

Failure Point Analysis

Reason 1: No Segmentation

Segmentation in Supernova is all or nothing. It's impossible to deliver exceptional service to every single client unless you segment and stay that way. 12/4/2 won't allow it, and your clients deserve it—it's what you promised. What happens at this failure point?

1. Too many clients to begin with.
2. Adding clients without eliminating others.
3. Poor execution of the min/max balance.

Min/Max

Min/max is something every advisor who has successfully segmented and implemented Supernova struggles with: keeping the right-sized segmented book at about the right size. That tension is a good thing—it's a sign of a thriving Supernova team. Remember, one of the model's core principles is acquisition of new clients and increasing growth year after year. That appears to directly conflict with the segmentation activities that we've already labeled as non-negotiable. So which is it?

A segmented book is a fluid, dynamic creature. The goal is to provide exceptional service to a sane and reasonable number of very deserving clients. While the number stays roughly the same, the faces change. And the mechanism for managing this state of existence is called *min/max,* or minimum and maximum.

The "maximum" is the number of clients a high-performing advisor and his or her support staff can consistently service with Supernova standards. In over seven years of coaching and observing Supernova FAs, the maximum number is about 100, with a handful of other clients who are part of the business because they just need to be: Maybe they are the parents of a major client, or essential to your acquisition program, or just the kind of person you need to accommodate if you plan on getting into heaven. You know who they are, but don't be too generous. Every client on this side list has a cost to your service commitments.

The "minimum" is where the growth is. It's the minimum size of investable assets that a client must have to be part of your Supernova flight, and every year it should climb higher.

As we will discuss in Chapter 6, a lively Supernova practice is continually seeking higher-balance clients who also fit the advisor's individual screens for what makes a client a Supernova client. Referrals and new business will find the successful Supernova practice. I've seen it happen countless times. I've also seen those same practices struggle with trying to accommodate the demands of an expanding client load. The truly generous solution is to graciously walk some clients to the door and wish them well.

Remember, your stated goal is exceptional service, and this isn't possible with an out-of-control book. The closet has room for only 20 suits.

Segmentation and Planning

Chapter 5 explores planning and how it has become the soul of every segmented Supernova practice. In fact, planning and segmentation are the yin and yang of Supernova. They give each other their shape. Segmentation creates the opening, so that genuine planning and effective implementation are possible. Planning creates such richness in the FAs workday that indiscriminate acquisition of new clients is not a temptation.

Grow the Team with the Business

Just as every FA's book is in a state of continual renewal, so too can be the firm's collective business. At Merrill, there was always a home for one of these segmented clients because there are multiple teams in every office. These clients deserve exceptional service, too—all do. So if one team can't provide it, it's also their responsibility to find another FA who can. Sometimes it's within their group, sometimes in their office, sometimes down the street.

For example, one Merrill FA has a fantastic relationship with a much smaller, independent advisor. She knows his investment model and knows he offers solid service. Her clients who drop below the minimum have been well served by this advisor. In turn, she has gained several clients who needed more than that office could provide. When everyone is working toward the same goal of providing exceptional service, good things happen naturally.

We've mapped out your first step along the invisible bridge. Up next is a practical guide to structuring your team and your workday in precise alignment with your clients' lives.

Leaps

Develop Your Inner Actuary

Supernova segmentation is about knowing exactly what clients pay you and what they cost you. Run a basic segmentation by production, and then look critically at the cost of that production. High-maintenance clients cost your practice in efficiency and, often, morale. The Supernova advisor has a crystal clear definition of who their ideal clients are. Who are yours?

Focus Your Discernment

Develop your own series of ever-smaller screens based on what you know about your business, your clients, and your values. George Kempf had 11 screens. What are yours?

Make the Change Productive For Everyone

Don't abandon the clients that don't make it through your segmentation; help them. Find an advisor that's right for them, and even develop other teams by introducing them to Supernova, and then coaching them. Taking care of your clients at this critical period can pay real dividends in referrals from other advisors and former clients. Segmentation is not only good for the advisory practice; it's good for the clients. Approach the process with a generous spirit. You couldn't help them the way they deserved to be helped. Whom can you introduce clients to, and why are they right for the job?

Maximum and Minimum

Set a maximum number of clients—100 is a proven number for a well-organized FA and his or her team. Also, set a minimum number of a client's total assets that you'll bring into your practice. Set them and stick to them. Supernova segmentation is not a fluid state. It's fixed and unmovable. Ultimately, you control who is in your book (see page 36), but successful FAs who use Supernova grow by lowering their maximum, raising their minimum, or both. Your max is 100. What's your minimum? Why?

Segment Everything

The exhilarating process of moving past unprofitable clients can inspire even more critical assessments, from the products you offer to the associations you belong to. What else can you segment in your practice?

CHAPTER 4

Organization

PROMISES MADE, PROMISES KEPT

In This Chapter

- Organization under Supernova is more than a to-do list. It's a major shift in operational practice.
- Organization under Supernova creates multiple opportunities for you to build trust. We call these deposits into the Bank of Trust.
- The Client Associate (CA) has the most important role in a well-organized Supernova team.
- Paper folders are fantastic tools that support exceptional client service in ways electronic systems cannot.
- The organization principles of Supernova are ideal documentation repositories for compliance purposes.
- When you are organized in Supernova, and following the 12/4/2 contact ritual, you are highly referable.

Organization in successful Supernova teams is about clear expectations and tight schedules. Time wasters, like telephone tag, are virtually eliminated.

Organization

If segmentation is Supernova's Big Bang, then organization is the next moment when the vast material of the universe is released and begins to take individual shape as galaxies, stars, and planets. And if each of those celestial bodies were clients under Supernova, they'd all be organized into folders. As you'll see, a real physical folder is the central piece of documentation in the Supernova service model.

Technology is a productivity enabler. So is guilt. In fact, guilt and obligation are two very old human responses that every new Supernova practice must learn to harness. The best teams we've seen have learned how to let guilt do its work until it became so embedded in the organizational DNA that it became culture.

And, no, that's not a Catholic joke.

Inverting the Org Chart

At Merrill, the Financial Advisors (FAs) are supported by Client Associates (CAs). In other organizations, these roles have different names but similar responsibilities. Being a CA is a big job in a Supernova practice because managers essentially toss them the keys to the car and tell them to get us where we need to be, please.

Under Supernova, the CA assumes a leadership role in the practice that is far more significant than ever before. They were important in the emergency room environment of the pre-Supernova practice, just like everyone with a pulse was important. Yet with Supernova, we were out to make them the day-to-day heartbeat of the business.

Are You Mental?

At Supernova rollouts, CAs asked us that very question, and some did not ask it as kindly. "How in the world, with all the work I have to do every day—all the emergencies, real and pretend—do you think I have time to schedule my FA's time? I can't even get to the bathroom, much less lunch." That statement reflected a very presegmentation mind-set, of course, but remember the first three stars of Supernova are tightly linked. We never talked about segmentation without organization and acquisition. So when they first heard that Supernova turned the organizational chart upside down and put the CA on top, they were right to ask: Were we mental?

No, but we were thinking hard.

We were thinking about 12/4/2 and how FAs were going to deliver the kinds of service we were promising to these newly identified ideal clients. See, the principles of the Supernova organization are the *natural extension of the 12/4/2 contact map.* Once FAs know that they are going to be interacting with their clients every month, the next questions are simple: What are we going to talk about, and when, exactly?

Supernova creates a team that lives to answer those questions. They know exactly what to talk about and exactly when. This brings us back to the folders and to guilt.

An Update on the "Permanent Record"

You remember permanent records from school or from your first job? The permanent record was a mythical thing that was believed to have great power in determining the very course of your life. It was not to be taken lightly. We loved that idea as Supernova was being born, so we borrowed the term.

In a Supernova organization, every client has a permanent record—a folder—and every time that client is on the phone or in the room, that folder is within reach. This folder doesn't contain every document or agreement. It's not where the tax returns or stock certificates are housed. But it is a comprehensive picture, on paper, of who that client is.

Specifically, the folder is both financial and personal, which are not so separate for the high-net-worth clients selected to be passengers on this first class flight. It's an evolving biography of the client's life as told to the FA and the CA. It contains an overall look at the assets under management, and the dreams that are behind those assets. It's about client's anniversaries, favorite movies, and where the grandkids are in school. There's an intimacy contained in the folder, and it's a powerful tool for delivering the exceptional client experience.

Think of the folder like a medical practice. You're the doctor and there's a patient waiting in the exam room. That's your client in there, waiting for the call. What does a doctor do? He or she picks up the folder that's in the bin outside the room, reviews it, brings it in, and uses its contents to help the patient. That folder is the record of observations, symptoms, prescriptions, and the diagnosis.

Here's another comparison: a dental office. The best of dental offices are pictures of professional efficiency, not because the dentist is so brilliant, but because the scheduler is so effective. The dentist knows that the practice makes money when the seats stay full, so he or she empowers the scheduler to make sure that happens. When was the last time you got a call from your dentist? Or say you needed to change an appointment; did you call the dentist personally? Doubt it. The administrator behind the desk runs most dental practices day to day.

The Low-Tech Silver Bullet

As Supernova began, we ran into the limitations of electronic contact systems such as ACT!. As mentioned in Chapter 3, ACT! was deeply integrated at Merrill but was too bulky and too vertical for Supernova. ACT! was also too easy to ignore because there was no "thump" as it landed on a desk. There was no guilt in just deleting a call entry that you never got around to making.

Every call, every meeting is tied to a low-tech client folder prepared by the CA. It's all the FA really needs to focus on, and if he or she doesn't get the calls made, there's an untouched folder right there asking "why?" But computers do it all better, you say? No. Networks crash, data disappears, and even when it's all up, it's just too easy to ignore. Folders are physical, not virtual. Clients have real lives and human needs. They deserve a service process that's just as alive.

Color Me Organized

Manila folders all look the same, which misses a fantastic opportunity to improve your Supernova organization. Try this: Green folders for client calls; blue for quarterly reviews; red for in-person meetings. Now keep them on a rack that stair-steps up so the colors of each are immediately evident. There's your day. Make the folders go away and know what it feels like to accomplish exactly what you set out to do.

A Day in the Life

Generally speaking, a FA who has 100 clients requires roughly 30 appointments a week or 6 appointments per day. The 6 appointments are 3 phone updates (20 minutes), 2 phone reviews (40 minutes), and 1 appointment in person (1 hour). That's only 3 hours and 20 minutes and would take up half of your day, leaving the other half for planning, prep time, and marketing.

The phone calls that don't include a quarterly review are 20 minutes each and have a limited agenda. For example, you may discuss an update on where the private-equity market is moving. These calls always begin with your asking the client, "Have there been any changes since the last time we talked?" If so, explore. It's their time, not yours. If they don't have much to say, cover your business and then hand the call back to the CA for scheduling. But before you do, always ask: "What was of value to you today?

What do you appreciate about our service to you?" In the chapters ahead, you'll see just how powerful those last questions can be.

The review calls are 40 minutes each and include a quarterly review. That conversation should end and sound a lot like the one above.

Some FAs like to plan their week with meetings and calls in the morning and planning and marketing in the afternoon. Others like this reversed. Others prefer to make all their calls in the first 10 days of the month and then focus the next 10 days of the month on marketing. Whatever works for you.

We've seen the best results when the FA has some updates, some phone reviews, and at least one appointment in person per day. That keeps you on the curve, or even ahead of it. A major source of frustration with Supernova is failure to keep up with the schedule, and that schedule is 100 percent the property of the CA.

The CA Owns the Calendar—Period

The CA organizes everything. The day's meetings and calls are on the calendar and have been for weeks or even months. Every client has been notified, reminded, and confirmed. (One of our teams sends a formal-looking appointment card through the mail for even telephone meetings. It works.)

Failure Point Analysis

Reason 2: Never Turning the Schedule Over to the CA

This is tough for some, easy for others. For everyone, it's critical. The CA runs the scheduling for the team, not just his or her schedule. And with the schedule responsibilities, this person claims the most important role on the team. They get the clients on the phone and in the office. They set the table for you to do what you do best—listen, advise, coach. You gain focus and provide efficient service by giving up control.

Each client has had their folder pulled and prepared by the CA. It can be a lot of work to prepare for a call. There's an agenda that builds on what was promised and discussed at previous appointments. But the focus of the call is to deliver real value—answers, knowledge, insight, relevant questions. It's not scripted, but it is organized, and the CA did all the organizing.

The FA moves from one call to the next, one meeting to the next, guided by the folders. Time for the 10:30 call with Mr. and Mrs. Martin? There's the folder: thump. If you don't make the call, the folder doesn't go away. It sits there and sits there, insisting with its physical presence that you pick up the phone and call. It will not be deleted. The good work of the CA can't easily be ignored without feeling—you guessed it—guilty.

Some of the genius of Supernova is evident in that moment. There's genius in the intersection of the physical folder and the very human need to do the right thing by the people working for you and with you.

Drucker Knew

If you haven't read Peter Drucker's quintessential guide to management, *The Effective Executive* (HarperCollins, 1967), add it to the list. If you have read it, it's worth another look if only to help you understand his ideas that reinforce Supernova organization. Drucker describes effectiveness as a habit—a ritual, in other words. He urges businesspeople to pay attention to where their time goes and build practices that focus on outcomes rather than the work required to reach them. He also connects effectiveness with concentrating on the few areas that will produce outstanding results. Yes! Drucker has observed that there are not 24 hours in a day, but only two or three. The difference between an executive who is effective and everyone else is the ability to use those hours effectively and "get the right things done."

The Bank of Trust: Now Accepting Deposits

Your client's trust is like an account; it can grow through deposits and be weakened by withdrawals. Too many withdrawals, and the account is in the red. There's a client looking for the door, as they should be. Trust makes everything else you do for them possible. Brilliant investing and flawless implementation of a perfect plan mean less for the relationship if the relationship is drawing on a low trust balance.

Supernova organization is a fabulous way to build up that trust account. With every call made exactly when scheduled, another deposit is made to the Bank of Trust. Another call, another deposit, and a growing balance ready to absorb the inevitable sudden withdrawal, otherwise known as a mistake.

You'll make mistakes because everyone does. Diagnosing and reducing them is ongoing and essential; eliminating them is impossible. So when they happen, the Bank of Trust account is rich enough to stay well in the black and compensate for your mistake.

Think of the folders as blank deposit slips to the Bank of Trust. Every time one goes from your desk back to the CA with the action completed, a deposit has been made. Get passionate about the folders. You'll learn to love their compelling simplicity almost as much as you hate telephone tag.

The Greatest Time Waster Ever: Phone Tag

An FA organized by Supernova simply doesn't waste time playing phone tag. When he or she picks up the phone, one of two things happens, both of which solve the phone tag problem: (1) The client is at the phone and ready, which happens a majority of the time—a true delight; or (2) the FA leaves a message that goes something like this: "Sorry we missed you. I had our appointment scheduled for today at 3:00. Please call [the CA] back to reschedule." That's it. The FA returns the folder and the CA is now in charge of rescheduling the call.

If the client does call back right away, the FA asks for the folder again and the call takes place. Some clients simply need another five minutes to finish whatever had them occupied, which makes quick return calls inevitable. Supernova organization is flexible, yet it's also very precise. Telephone tag is the opposite of precision—it's random, it's unpredictable, it's a waste of time.

In fact, most incoming calls are distracting and disruptive. The high-performance Supernova team receives far fewer client calls than they make. Said one FA, a year into Supernova, with amazement in her voice: "My phone hardly ever rings." Now that's a sweet sound.

The Greatest Time-Saver Ever: Batch Processing

One of our FA's clients, a manufacturer of boat propellers, taught the FA an important lesson about productivity: Do similar things at the same time. He called it "batch processing." The FA had already created a financial plan for his 211 clients, each with 211 sets of varied needs. His "aha" moment came when he connected the similar needs of each client—insurance, estate planning, income—and created a contact plan around those topics. Now for one month on his 12/4/2, he is almost solely focused on one common need. Although this might appear to be a depersonalized plan, it is actually an effective way to deliver personalized services more efficiently. For example, when mortgage rates are right for one client, they are right for many other clients. If one client's insurance is out of whack, chances are other clients are, too. It's batch processing elevated to the Supernova level.

Ritual over Discipline

In a Supernova organization, the wisdom of enacting rituals over forcing discipline is especially evident. We introduced this idea in Chapter 2, and it needs amplification here.

You don't think about rituals—getting up, brushing your teeth, taking a shower. It just happens. Same with client contact in a Supernova practice. You come in, look over your folders, make the calls, write the notes, put the folders away. It becomes a ritual. You're not thinking about the process any more than you think about the toothbrush. If you're engaged, you're thinking in a focused way on the client and how to enhance their life and help them reach their goals.

Creative insights are the product of minds that are free to make associations between separate facts and concepts. It's been said an idea is a feat of association, not a flash of brilliance. We have observed this often.

We've seen FAs prosper because their day was so well planned that they could devote nearly all their intuition and awareness to their clients. There was no reaction to a crisis or a noncrisis. There was no energy devoted to playing catch-up on a day that had slipped away. The day's goals have the simple clarity of a yard that needs mowing: You see it, you begin, you stay with it, you finish it. Now look back on the fresh cut turf. That's the satisfaction that marks a day with Supernova.

Think about what makes you tired at the end of a typical day. Chances are it's not the work you completed, it's the work you *didn't* get done that saps your mental energy. So what invigorates you then? It's what you accomplished; it's the yard you mowed. That's work, too, but satisfying and rewarding. The days go incredibly fast in a Supernova practice; the difference is that nearly every minute is devoted to creating an exceptional client experience.

Golfers and Compliance Officers

It's a good thing that the financial advisory business is disclosing more and working even harder to comply with securities regulations. Clients deserve it. Advisors are getting used to it. Compliance officers are demanding clear and readily available documentation on what goes on between a client and the firm. Supernova organization wasn't built for compliance, but it sure delights the compliance officer to see such organized and comprehensive records.

At Merrill, the compliance leadership became vocal advocates of Supernova. They know the FA's legal vulnerabilities better than most of us, and the weapons they use against lawsuits, frivolous or not, are documents. Supernova folders, which contain every call and follow-up letters that restate responsibilities, actions, and open questions, provide that documentation.

And lest you think that the Supernova advisors are inflexible service-bots, consider this: The most together FAs schedule their time off with the same efficiency as their time on. Want to play a round every other Friday afternoon? Build a schedule that accommodates it and do it. Don't skulk around trying to sneak out or resent it when unplanned work intrudes. All work is unplanned unless you plan all of it.

Failure Point Analysis

Reason 3: Failure to Adhere to a Schedule

The CA and FA are in a dance, and like any dance, it takes two. If the CA is doing the job of scheduling client calls, and the FA is not making the calls, Supernova will fail. This one shows itself in a hurry, too. Nothing will drain the energy from a hardworking CA like an FA who is not showing up. We've heard it before: "We tried that Supernova thing but it just didn't work." No, my friend, you didn't. Don't let it fail by not pulling your weight.

"It's What We Are Referred On"

There are a few other aspects of Supernova's principle of organization I want to touch on because they lead right into another component of the model: acquisition. Let's hear from one of the most successful practices I've seen. Listen to how their contact model became what this group is referred on:

> After a while, the clients began to realize we were giving them better service . . . real service. And you can argue we

are always giving them service, but the point is the client didn't understand there was a new agreement. We promised to give them something, and we delivered. And so what began to happen is we really would go out and have much more meaningful structured meetings and conversations on our telephone calls.

What I never dreamed would happen is this: Those scheduled calls are the number one way that clients introduce us to prospective clients. "They're going to call you every month and they're going to have two face-to-face meetings," and on down the line.

And so as clients introduce us to other clients, they don't introduce us as their asset managers or the guys who pick my stocks. They introduce us as the people who quarterback our financial lives and that we talk to every month. It's a real differentiator, and we began to use it as a marketing strategy.

The FAs in that practice also have seen that the first 90 days of a relationship are when they are especially referable. In the next chapter, we'll learn more about how they structure that critical period. Right now, though, that same group also does something that demonstrates the major role of the CA to the client. I love how this CA is immediately seen as the go-to person for detail and document questions, not the FA. The perception is fixed from the first session once a client is a client:

We want that meeting not to be run by the FA, but by the CA, so the CA and client have the opportunity to get to know each other and then the client understands that we are not, as partners, in the paperwork business. We're in the advisory business and wealth management business, so we'll sit down together and they'll go over the paperwork, and it cements that relationship. So anytime they want something that is more administrative, they're not going to go to a partner; they're going to go to the CA. That's worked really well and we have gotten some nice feedback from the client. They appreciate the directness. They don't want to waste our time any more than we want to waste theirs.

Leaps

Let Voice Mail Work for You, Not the Other Way

The intent of Supernova organization is not to turn you into a call center. It's a structure that allows for deeper connections and greater creativity. Try this for one week: Put an outgoing message that says you'll be returning calls at 11:00 AM and 4:00 PM. Let your clients and team know you are available for emergencies and truly urgent issues, and they can reach you through the CA. Then send every single call into voice mail. Keep your promise with return calls, but don't listen to messages beforehand. At the end of the week, evaluate your productivity and your focus.

Manage the Drip-Drip-Drip of Constant E-mails

E-mail can erode your effectiveness under the guise of being effective. Don't let it. Turn it off except when you are ready to read and respond with your full focus.

Know Thyself

Supernova's folder system exists in the context of the technological tools and environments that support the modern-day FA. The key is knowing yourself. Can you blend an electronic contact management system with the 12/4/2 contact ritual and the intimacy and empathy that makes it relevant to your clients? For every FA, there's a sweet spot where the technology tools and the physical presence of the folders combine for exceptional service to the clients. Find yours.

Turn Over the Wheel

A Supernova organization puts the CA at the top of the chart. This is an empowering move not only for the CA, but for the entire practice.

CHAPTER

Planning

INSPIRED ACTION

In This Chapter

- Planning is what you're hired to do.
- In Supernova, planning means deep client knowledge and purposeful action. It's not in a binder, or even in a certification.
- Supernova advisors can become a chief financial officer (CFO) for their clients.
- The 12/4/2 contact ritual is how you implement the plan.
- Planning is based on values, not just increasing value.
- Implementing the plan also means coaching the client.

From where your clients are, the planning star in Supernova is the most evident and most important. They will appreciate (and maybe marvel at) your organization, but they will trust you and remain loyal because of your planning.

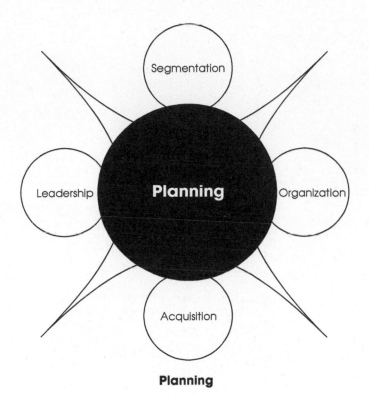

Planning

In the seven years that I coached Supernova practices, and in the several hundred client meetings I observed that were led by Supernova advisors, I've never once heard a prospective or current client say this: I want Supernova.

They want access to your expertise so that they can grow and preserve their wealth—not miracles, but certainly mastery. They want exceptional service, because chances are they've experienced the other kind. They want to be heard and understood. They want a vision of their financial life, and they need help turning that vision into reality.

Did you see anything in there about wanting to be part of a segmented practice? Or hoping that you'll call them every month? Or wanting to share a bunch of high-quality referrals? Of course not. Supernova itself is not what the Supernova practice is offering. Supernova is the platform for what you're actually hired on: guidance, wisdom, empathy, collaboration, coaching, vigilance, help.

What Money *Can't* Buy

In the book, *Money and the Meaning of Life: Spiritual Search in a Material World* (Bantam Doubleday Dell, 1991), Jacob Needleman affirms what you've always felt and yet still manages to surprise you. He asks the question, "What's the one thing money can't buy?" Happiness? Good health? Love? While these answers are true sometimes, they are not universal. Money can buy the experiences that let happiness and even love rise in us. Often, good health is relative to money. For example, if two people had the exact same illness, who do you think is more likely getting the better care? The patient with money. So what is the one thing money can't buy?

Needleman writes that, universally and throughout time, the one thing money can't buy is meaning. That statement is brilliant, both as an insight, and as an opportunity for the Supernova FA.

The opportunity of Supernova is in the demographics, specifically the Baby Boomers. People in this generation have been driving cultural change from the moment they bought their first Elvis single. Boomers threw their idealistic energy at civil rights and Vietnam. When they had kids, they willed the mini-van into existence, and later, in their middle age, they keep pharmaceutical companies in the black and on TV. With their passion and their purchases, Baby Boomers have been changing the world for four decades. They want to change it now, too, and they have the wealth to do it. Enter the Supernova FA.

Beyond Binders

You've seen them. Oh heck, you've probably even generated a few. Big Important Documents with custom covers and color-coded tabs. Some advisors call that overloaded binder their plan and consider its contents their planning. Given all the trees that gave their lives for it, you'd think the people behind it would put some of their lives into it as well. Unfortunately, that is rarely the case. That's not true planning.

These lifeless binders have also lost their ability to impress clients, too. Clients have endured all the questions and dug up all the documents that go into the so-called plan, and then they have seen their binder just sit there, inert and lifeless. They want a plan, and they've learned what true planning is not. So what is it?

True planning is a synthesis of financial acumen, customer intimacy, creative thinking, life coaching, personal training, and team culture. It's the full plate of what an evolved advisory practice offers, and it's what they grow their business on.

Planning Is Meaning with Deadlines

Imagine client conversations that set out to answer these kinds of questions:

- Rate your overall happiness, from 1 to 10. Where are you? Where do you want to be?
- Think of a time when you were genuinely happy and fully engaged as a person. What were you doing? Let's explore what we can do now to ignite those feelings once again.
- What do you enjoy? Now, what gives you joy? The difference between them may help us create a plan that moves beyond merely enjoying yourself to creating a fully joyous life.
- What's your financial legacy? What is the legacy of your values? Let's brainstorm on a plan that leverages your wealth so that it creates a legacy far greater than dollars.

Now try fitting all of that that into a binder. You can't.

Planning and Implementation: Joined at the Hip

Throughout this chapter and the book, with every reference to planning we are insisting on a broader definition: planning and implementation. There are the conversations and the research and the recommendations. That's the plan. Then there's the 12/4/2 contact, more conversations, and sharp execution. That's implementation. As we said in the previous chapter, 12/4/2 is almost exclusively devoted to implementing the plan. This is an essential understanding.

Notice that I didn't say *plan* or *planner* for reasons you can probably guess. Those terms are inherently static—fixed in time or locked into a role. Planning may seem like an old-fashioned notion in the fast-forward world of financial instruments. But by expressing a true planning ethic, and doing it year on year on year, you can create something far more important than beating the S&P this quarter. It's called a legacy.

Planning Meets Organization

This elevated model of planning, which is in fact a true advisory practice, is in perfect sync with Supernova's principle of organization. This synchronization gives the contact ritual of 12/4/2 something to work with. It's where the action items of a well-tuned plan intersect with the dynamics of a well-run client relationship.

In the early days of a client relationship, there's a lot to accomplish. It will take several months to work through what the plan presents as remedies and tactics. Discussions with the certified public accountant (CPA), the estate-planning attorney, and the insurance agents all need to be scheduled and planned for. The portfolio allocations need to be dialed in, with increasing insight to the tax efficiencies and risk tolerances, none of which takes place in a week—nor should it.

By bringing the action items of a plan into alignment with Supernova's contact rituals and organized folders, they occur in the right order and have the highest likelihood of actually being the right solutions.

Think Estate Planning, Not CFP

Certified Financial Planners (CFPs) can do wonderful work for high-net-worth clients when they transcend the plan document and create meaningful action. The best of them have mastered the minutia of the financial instruments *and* possess a deep knowledge of the client's dreams. If you find one, hire them. If you *are* one, your moment is now.

More common (although not as much as clients deserve) is the evolved estate planner. At their best, these pros are focused on real lives and real issues, not documents or the alphabet soup of trusts. Exceptional estate planners know all the tools, but a conversation with them has more questions and "what ifs?" than acronym-laden answers.

Okay, here's one acronym worth using: CFO.

Your Family CFO

That's how Chris Brooke and Rita McCluskey frame it, and it's working spectacularly. Their practice, Brooke, McCluskey & Associates, is one of the most successful in their area. Chris says:

> We say the same thing to every prospective client. When you work with us, you're the CEO and we're the CFO. They usually get it right away. You can see it in their eyes. We are hired to run their financial life like it was a business. We hold a broad view and we bring in outside resources as necessary. The CFO analogy really resonates because it suggests both our competence and how we work.

Fabulous. The family CFO creates a powerful narrative in the client's mind: This person is an expert who manages a team, saves me money, and reports to me. The clients know what a CFO does, and they can easily imagine what one might be able to do for them. But the even better news is that the clients don't know the half of it.

The Brooke/McCluskey family CFO is *not* the pampered executive type who sits behind a mahogany desk and fires off one of equally wooden memos. No, these "CFO's" are the best planning practices we have ever had the pleasure to coach. They've coached us, in fact. Imagine what they do for their clients. Here's what Rita said:

> Our initial planning process does generate a document. There's a lot of data that has to reside somewhere, but we don't spend much time on it. The plan to us is the list of action items we develop—that's the real deliverable of this first step. These are specific activities we intend to focus on as we move the client closer and closer to their goals—goals they have shared with us, and we have teased out of them through some pretty gut-level kinds of conversations.

Action items and gut-level conversations. Is my definition of planning starting to come to life for you? Once more, here are Chris and Rita:

> **Chris:** We put a lot of team time into each initial planning. We actually charge a fee because we believe there is a great deal of value for the client even if they don't hire us. If nothing else, they've seen what our level of planning looks like and that helps them make a better choice, even if they don't choose us.
>
> **Rita:** Or if we don't choose them. And *team time'* is the right term, too. Twice during the development of an initial plan we get the full team together. First to meet the client, usually over lunch or dinner, where we ask a lot of questions and just generally get to know one another. Do we like them as people? Do we think we can help them? Then once we've worked up a draft plan, we all get together again and brainstorm on action items. Very open-ended, blue sky stuff, and time consuming.
>
> **Chris:** It's a huge commitment, but we do it because it works. It helps the client see how we operate so they know what to expect, and it gives us the solid base of understanding that lets us implement with passion. Our action items call for client action too, which means we're going to be pushing these folks on occasion. If we don't truly believe it's for their own good, we're not going to be as effective.

Clearly, these are not your father's planners.

Planning Deepens and Protects Your Relationship

At its heart, developing a plan is a conversation between you and your clients, even between your client's present and your client's future. These conversations are rich and meaningful *and rare*. They just don't happen much, but when you can generate them, you are establishing an intimacy that makes you indispensable. "Own the plan and own the relationship," the saying goes, and it's true as long as the plan is being implemented. And after a few years of well-organized

People don't remember what you say, or what you do. But if they feel loved in your presence, they will remember you forever.

Mother Teresa

and effective implementation, you will have established a force-field around your client that competing advisors will probably never be able to penetrate.

Investing as Nonhero

You'll notice the particulars of an advisor's investment model haven't shown up much. Of course, that's intentional. I'm assuming your investment strategies are informed, intelligent, and appropriate. You're a brilliant investment strategist, and I don't care.

Okay, I care about it just as much as I care about your team's ability to, say, bring a selection of killer CPAs to the table to find the right one for your client. You get the point. Your investment model is not the most important thing you're offering, nor is it the least. Asset growth strategies are tightly integrated into the action items generated by the plan.

The Supernova business model is about creating exceptional client experiences and transforming those experiences into growth. Know where your investment success resides within that, and you'll have it positioned about right. However, there is a skill that you might not have developed nearly as well as Supernova demands.

The Coach: You

This is one of the most exciting observations so far. We've seen a number of Supernova advisors transform themselves as coaches to their clients. It's a genuine paradigm shift as thrilling in its implications for the advisor as it is responsible to the client.

These relationships have gone past the traditional (and limiting) roles of the advisor and the advised. While client intimacy and action-oriented planning are essential here, it's *coaching* that animates them.

The advisors I've seen in these coaching roles are absolute delights to watch and learn from. Their client relationships are on another level. They are both informal and highly informed. They have a way of getting the most out of everyone they touch, especially their clients. And clients' response to them? Pick one: Trust. Respect. Loyalty. And this one: Commitment.

Clients who have been expertly coached in their financial lives are committed partners in seeing the relationship succeed. Not just their own financial lives, but the very relationship with the advisor as well. The best analogy is a great personal trainer who takes your aerobic, weight loss, or muscle-building progress personally. They're invested in you. They have expectations of you. They're good for you. So you commit to them because you see how much they've committed to you, and, consequently, that commitment ends up as success.

> *Even the rich are hungry for love, for being cared for, for being wanted, for having someone to call their own.*
> *Mother Teresa*

Rita has a story that wraps this point up, and leads us to another core component of planning:

> I offered to sit in on a meeting between one of our larger clients and his attorney to review some trust documents. As the review proceeded, I saw that some of the distribution, if it occurred today, would go to his daughter's potential ex-spouse as part of the marital estate. There was a great deal of disharmony in that marriage, and a divorce was likely. I'd been talking a lot with the client about this situation and what we could do to anticipate it, both financially and emotionally. So I pointed out the distribution and the attorney confirmed it. The changes were initiated that very day, and as we were leaving, the client asked me to please sit in on every meeting from then on with his attorney or

CPA. We can't do this for every client, but he was one of our best. He committed to our plan and he referred us often.

Commitment inspires deeper commitment. It's a tough promise for Rita to keep, yet how many clients like this do you need? Not many, because each one is worth so much.

Three Kinds of Supernova Teams

The Blended Team: Here's the "before": a decent stock picker with a big book; a good bond broker with loyal and satisfied customers, but only for their bonds; and a strong money manager with good client skills, but no planning chops. Here's the "after": Same three, with appropriate Supernova segmentation, disciplined organization, and the addition of two top planners with solid investment processes. Client calls became planning sessions, which became real plans. Heretofore unknown assets poured in. Client satisfaction soared.

The Tag Team: Planning and a sound investment process go hand in hand. This two-person Supernova team demonstrated what can happen when a knowledgeable planner with a passion for helping clients enhance all financial possibilities aligns with an advisor with a bulletproof investment process. So what happened? A meteoric rise in production and client satisfaction.

The Meticulous Team: This could be the Supernova poster team. Not because they get spectacular results (they do, of course), but because they get those results through a meticulous and precise implementation of the full Supernova model. They work straight from the recipe, and are a machine of Supernova efficiency and growth. Not surprisingly, planning is a core skill.

The Family Office, Reimagined

A planning-oriented Supernova advisor can do something else remarkable besides coach the client to higher levels of success. They can also coach the other advisors who serve them.

It's the same principle—a high-level collaboration that elevates everyone involved.

Take the CPA, for example. We discuss in Chapter 6 how bringing potential CPAs into a review makes a lot of good things happen. Let's say the client is delighted with their current CPA, or that the CPA you helped them hire is now on the job. If the relationship never proceeds past professional courtesy, then all you're doing is sharing documents—and missing opportunities.

Let's imagine another way of working that is active and transparent—one that positions you as the coach of a multidisciplinary team. Winning isn't measured by how much the client trusts you, but by how much *you are willing to give for the client.* The CPA says he is committed, and he may be. Great. Build on that with actions that model what a deeper commitment looks like. Then see what it inspires in the client.

By bringing all the advisors—the CPA, the various attorneys, and insurance pros—into a turf-free dialogue, you are bringing an entirely new business entity to life: the virtual family office. We've seen a few of these develop, and they are wonders. Clients are served by a team and a collective commitment that is creative, active, and perfectly in line with their goals. What does it take? Just everything you've got.

Let's take the next step to acquisition. Client acquisition is built into Supernova's core principles. The advisory team that segments and organizes, but never grows or grows at a plodding, uneven pace, is something less than a Supernova team.

Leaps

Conversation Pays

In the book, *Blink* (Little, Brown and Company, 2005) the wise Malcolm Gladwell explores why some doctors get sued for malpractice at higher rates than others. The difference? Doctors who do not get sued make so-called orienting comments like "After the exam, we'll talk the problem over and I'll leave time for your questions" part of the patient/doctor conversations. These doctors are also characterized as having gentle humor and encourage clients to tell them more. There was no difference in the quality of care or the amount of what the doctor shared. And all this empathy took a total of three minutes extra in conversation—15 minutes versus 18 minutes for the doctors who had never been sued. The lesson to be learned: Be a better conversationalist. Learn how to listen, while being actively engaged. Practice with your team. Get a coach. You'll have a better plan and a deeper relationship. Conversation pays.

Aristotle as Supernova Advisor

In "On Rhetoric," Aristotle defined three specific pathways, or "modes" for a person to connect with his or her audience. Your client is your audience. Here's how Aristotle would coach you: Show your character, stir their emotion, prove your truth. Or in ancient Greek-speak: ethos, pathos, logos.

Ethos is your character, defined in details large and small. It's better earned than talked about, but if you don't have it, your effectiveness as a planner can be limited.

Pathos is generated by sharing some of yourself. The emotions at the center of a client's unspoken dreams can be unlocked by sharing your own dreams. Reveal something real, and you'll often be gifted with the same.

Logos is contained in the data points and trend lines. It's powerful when used in combination, but ineffective when trying to reach core values and build a plan around them.

So the next time you are with a client, keep Aristotle in the room, and see if you can bring awareness and then mastery to how you weave ethos, pathos, and logos into your conversations.

Planning is Coaching

The image of a book-smart CFP doesn't match up with an involved personal coach, but the Supernova advisor needs to find a way to inhabit both. It begins with how the plan is constructed. Use action words and commit yourself and your client to specific actions and deadlines. Financial plans can drift into the abstract, which makes them inherently difficult to implement. Keep them alive and snappy, and you'll have a plan that's more coachable.

CHAPTER 6

Acquisition

EXPLOSIVE GROWTH UNDER CONTROL

In This Chapter

- Supernova is, first and foremost, about growth—controlled, intentional and continuous.
- Growth occurs by raising your minimum asset threshold, not just by acquiring more clients.
- Develop and coach a set of advisory teams for the clients who fall out of your minimum asset requirements.
- Cold calls can lead to business, especially when they deliver value, but exceptional service is what you must leverage as a driver of growth.
- Develop growth strategies that cast your current clients as advisors. They can become invested in your growth.
- Develop a vertical specialization. Become "Slightly Famous."
- Develop professional networking with the aim of guiding your clients to better service.
- Every major activity is scheduled in Supernova, including your prospecting and business development.

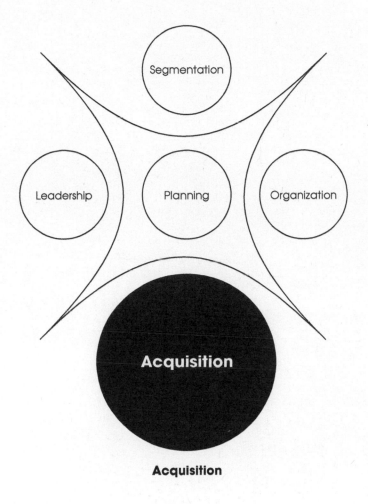

Acquisition

A true Supernova practice is a growing practice. The acquisition star is continually burning. It feeds off the energy created by the other stars, without diminishing them.

Don't be misled by what you read in the previous chapters. Supernova may have been born to rescue our floundering FAs from their desperate and self-limiting environments that were overladen by clients, but it lives and *thrives* in the model's fourth star: acquisition. If segmentation and organization are the science of Supernova, acquisition is the art. And in this chapter, we're going to create it.

Supernova Is Growth

While Supernova accomplishes many things, all of them good, the only real reason to adopt it is to grow your practice. Growth is what gets you to take that first leap of faith onto the invisible bridge. We saw this evidenced in the early days as the model spread throughout Merrill. One FA said, "I would not have had the courage to end a client relationship if I wasn't absolutely convinced I could grow my business in a controlled way."

We also see the desire for controlled growth when coaching newer teams who are essentially only operating under Supernova. They can't imagine that the service and organizational aspects of the model were ever even discussed independently of acquisition. Good for them. Here are three things both groups know.

Supernova Creates Time to Grow

By organizing your client contact down to the hour, you also create the space in your week to devote to business development—be it referrals or prospecting. And the correlation is direct, too. A Supernova Advisor who spends 20 percent of his or her week focused on actively acquiring new relationships will grow the business by 20 percent.

Exceptional Service Is What Makes You Referable

A major disconnect in some advisory practices is asking for referrals without making sure they are referable. Be referable first. It's basic, but essential. How can an advisor expect referrals, much less have the moxie to ask for them, if they haven't delivered exceptional service?

Developing Referrals Is More than Asking

Referrals are generated through a process that is practiced, managed, coached, and measured. It's more than asking. It's also more than a script. An effective referral process is an extension of your respectful relationship with your client and is characterized by two foundations: humility and candor.

Growth in a Minimum/Maximum Environment

As you read earlier, a pure Supernova practice grows in one way and one way only—by raising the minimum level of assets or production it takes to get on the first-class plane. That's the goal of all acquisition efforts—raise the minimum, don't add past your maximum. Yet how can you expect your clients, who know the basics of your business model (in other words, all of them), to be comfortable knowing they are in the low ranges of your minimum asset level?

Here's how.

Everyone wants (and deserves) first-class service. So the best way to accommodate clients who don't qualify for your first-class flight is to have another team all trained and ready to offer them the same or *even better service* than they can get on your flight. One team uses this line while deferred clients go to another all-trained team:

> Our team is growing, and my focus is shifting. We will not be able to deliver the level of service that you have become accustomed to. That being said, I'd like to introduce you to another team. They're doing everything that we're doing. They're fabulous. Let's meet them and see if there's a fit. You'll be a priority client to them, and I will personally supervise the migration and be available to you at any time during the transition.

"They Don't Have Enough Money for You"

That may be true, so listen carefully and probe a bit more. They also might be hesitating because they simply don't want to expose their friends to rejection because they don't hit your minimum. One FA team has a great response. "Our commitment to you is this: If you refer us to someone you know, and they want to meet us, we will talk with them for at least an hour to explore if it's a good fit. If not, we'll recommend another team we're confident in.

The Mantra: Service and Growth

Supernova drives practice growth in three ways. The first way is through higher client satisfaction and loyalty. This, in turn, leads to attracting more assets—that's an automatic occurrence when the advisor delivers on the promises made in a Supernova organization.

The other two drivers for growth are referrals and smarter market positioning, both of which are propelled forward by the service you've already delivered. Service drives growth. A practice may be a wonderful collection of organized professionals and a dream come true for a select group of very fortunate clients, but if it's not growing quickly and with control, it's not a Supernova practice.

Clearly, growth is deeply integrated into the warrior mind-set common in financial services. I've encountered some ferocious fighters during my career, and I've also seen how their voraciousness can work against them and their practices.

Supernova gives advisors of all mind-sets—from the reserved planner to the gregarious hunter—an advantage they have been lacking. It's called the ultimate client experience, and like all effective weapons, it serves to both attack and defend.

Service Creates a Force Field

Exceptional client service builds comfort, and comfort leads to intimacy. It's not about mere friendship. It's about the environment that is created by an ongoing dialogue between an FA and his client about the client's needs, wants, and desires. It's also about an FA delivering on the promises made with modesty and warmth. Create this type of environment, and you will grow a forcefield around your clients that quickly and quietly wards off any competitive approaches or firms. One FA said, "I knew my client was constantly getting approached by calls and letters from other advisors. 'No thanks,' they said. 'We're very, very pleased with our advisor.'"

Service Turns the Conversation

In a conversation with a prospective client, especially one not developed through a referral, the specific details of Supernova service should be front and center. Let the other so-called advisors blather on about their investment model and their record of outperforming the S&P. Every firm has great charts, and every wealthy person has already seen it. Don't get me wrong, they care about their money, but they also know that asset growth is only one reason to hire you, and, as discussed earlier, it may not be the best one.

Instead, talk to prospective clients about the 12/2/4 contact ritual. Tell them about first-class service for a tightly controlled client roster. Wax poetic about folders. We've watched FAs do just this, and then ask politely, "Now how does this compare to the service you're currently enjoying?" The reactions typically range from a dismissive snort to an outright howl. Apparently, there are a lot of service-challenged advisors out there. Advantage: you. Now, how do you use it to grow your business? It begins with referrals.

The Referral Mind-set

Here's the mind-set for harvesting great referrals: Your clients are part of your business development team. Clients should know your growth strategy because you've told them. (The sharpest business-minded clients will want to know anyway, because every client wants to work for a prospering firm.) Clients should also know your minimum/maximum. Based on this knowledge, they probably have a good idea of what kinds of people would be a good fit in your book. So give your clients a role and set some gentle expectations.

Existing clients who are dialed into your model and who are ready to refer you are like the matchmakers from the Old World—respected and cared for. Make it clear that by helping your firm grow, you will keep them on board, even if that growth raises your minimum past their asset level. That's a gift for their referral services.

We've seen spectacular growth from Supernova teams that had tight referral processes and let their clients take appropriate ownership of the team's growth.

Putting Wheels on the Best Ideas

We've seen hundreds of referral techniques, from the elegant to the intrusive. "Who do you know that I can call" is what many referral processes boil down to. You can do better. Supernova teams create shared ownership of growth while also reinforcing their commitment and loyalty to clients. Supernova creates truly unique value. It's your job as a growing team to leverage it.

In hundreds of teams we've taken the strongest referral processes we've encountered and dropped them onto a Supernova track. We've also developed a few of our own. Here's a primer.

Think Marketing, Not Sales

Author, consultant, and coach Richard Weylman has a lot to say on how financial advisors to the affluent need to raise their game out of the sales vernacular and into the marketing environment. He says, "Sales keep you in business, but marketing keeps you in sales." Richard's book, *Opening Closed Doors: Key to Reaching Hard-To-Reach People*, is a must read.

Richard was consistently on stage with us as we rolled out Supernova because his model of marketing over sales fit perfectly with the acquisition principle of Supernova. Richard knows that to be effective in the affluent market, advisors need to develop their brands—positioning their firm before promoting it.

A position in the market is what you become famous for. It could be a specialization, like entrepreneurs or corporate attorneys. It could be a high visibility among cultural or charitable leaders. It could simply be your exceptional service and your comprehensive, action-oriented planning. That's what marketers do. They position companies so that effective selling can take place. As Richard says, "Your clients want to buy solutions, not products. Marketers focus on people's needs. Merchandisers focus on products."

VIPS

In his book *Get More Referrals Now!* (McGraw Hill, 2004), Bill Cates presents the VIPS process. Listen in on the sample client meeting I imagined below and see if you can connect the dots, or in this case, the words that comprise the meaning of VIPS:

You're in one of your review meetings, in person, not on a call, though calls can provide similar opportunities. The meeting begins like they all should: big picture and blue sky. What's happening in your life? Your family? Your work or retirement? What are you excited about or uneasy about? Put it all on the table. Take good notes. Add them to the folder. Respond effectively. Now it's your turn to talk.

"Last time we talked these were the open issues, here's where we are. . . ." Or "our plan tells us that this month we need to review the estate, and make sure all the securities are appropriately titled. . . ." You get the idea. It's when you do the business of a financial advisory firm. Wrap it up when it's over, but you're not done.

Question: "What did you value from the experience today?" A simple question focused on *their* experience not your performance. They'll answer it too. "It's how much you care." Or "it's how organized you are." Or "it's our friendship." If it's true for them, it's the answer you wanted to hear. And once it's established: "What I want to talk about next is very important. With your permission, I'd like to do some brainstorming, just you and me."

The focus of that brainstorming is to connect the value they have just identified with anyone else they think might benefit from that value. Not the 11 other things 11 other clients value, but that one thing. Start there, return there, see where the discussion takes you. You are defining their role in your growth. Be grateful. "I really appreciate your suggestions."

So what are the words that make up Cates's VIPS concept? Value. Important. Permission. Suggestions. VIPS. Great stuff because it makes a seamless connection to your value. Even if your client came up blank, they had the chance to revisit and restate what keeps you around. Of course, a Supernova advisor also anticipates the occasional shrugs and sheepish response.

Supernova Cold Calls: Stay Valuable

Cold calls have a bad reputation and have earned it, too. But they're not all bad. If you bring a Supernova mind-set to your cold calls, they can help you grow strategically. Who you're calling matters—that's the strategic part—yet the most important aspect is what you're offering when they answer. Make the call mean something to a high-net-worth individual; share some insight into donor-managed funds or capital gains taxes. Changes in the tax code provide a continuous opportunity to educate, inform, and impress prospects. Make it a gift that they can act on, or investigate, without hiring you. This combination of expertise and empathy can make a fantastic first impression and sets the table nicely for the level of service you are prepared to give if they become a Supernova client.

Go to the Folder

Client folders are rich with potential referrals. In order to maximize their potential, you must start thinking that way from day one. As you gather the essential information on your client, take a few minutes to fill out the picture. Get information on your client's family members and note their situation briefly: "My brother, oh, he's in the diaper delivery business." Whatever. Get it all. Get information on their business partners, their life coach, their doctor, their lawyer, their CPA, and so on (more on that later). For example, you may ask:

> "What about your brother? Is he still in the baby business? That's always growing, do you think our value to you might also resonate with him?"
>
> "How about your former partner? Have you stayed in contact?"

You don't need to drag the session down with addresses and zodiac signs, but make sure you get a name and his/her relationship to your client. It's the first step toward true client intimacy and it has its own rewards: It creates a rich image of your client's life. When you know more about the people in their life, then you can prompt them when they can't think of a single person who might benefit from your value.

Use the initial (and always evolving) folder as a base that you return to again and again for referrals. The most incisive and helpful clients will see exactly what you're doing. They will develop their own lists—people who might not have occurred to them if you hadn't expanded their thinking.

There are two more referral strategies to unpack: The first is about going vertical; the second is about developing the golden Rolodex. (For those of you reading quickly, that was Rolodex, the contact holder—not Rolex, the watch. But nail your acquisition, and it's just a matter of time until you'll have both.)

Beautiful. Right away, you've sidestepped the hesitation and promised to deliver the same kind of service you are famous for in the client's mind. You've also told your client in very clear terms that you take their referrals seriously enough to invest an hour in each one. If they understand your contact system, they know the significance of that commitment. Chances are that the quality of their referrals will reflect it. That's keeping your clients on your referral team.

Diving in Vertically

Vertical specialization is a growing business trend that means the advisor has become recognized for his or her expertise within a narrowly defined market. Steven Van Yoder refers to going vertical as "Getting Slightly Famous" in his book *Get Slightly Famous* (Bay Tree Publishing, 2003). Vertical specialization in any advisory firm tends to happen organically and over time. A lawyer who does great work for a mortgage company tends to get more business from mortgage companies, until one day he looks around his practice and realizes he's a mortgage law specialist. Supernova advisors aren't quite so passive—at least, not Tony Singh.

Tony built a profitable subspecialty by serving anesthesiologists. These high-net-worth professionals are a huge part of his revenue. He's even written articles for their publications and presented at conferences. Tony built this part of his business partly on referrals, some solicited and many more unsolicited. The savvy vertical marketing tactics that positioned him within the anesthesiologist market continue to serve him well, yet the secret to his success with these hard-to-reach professionals has more to do with being humble than smart. Here's what Tony said:

> After we segmented the practice we identified several anesthesiologists who were very good clients. They had solid production, consistent asset growth, and were generally good people. I thought there was room for more of these folks in my book so I started exploring using Larry Biederman's "SMART Marketing" technique. At its core, it's a simple question: "If you were me and trying to build your business with anesthesiologists, what would you do?"

What Tony heard varied from client to client—some references, some marketing advice, some ideas on how to tune his service model to better accommodate them. It was all gold, even if not all of it was the right advice for Tony. Because what was happening there was the core insight of this chapter: *Position your clients to take ownership in your growth.*

As Tony's list of anesthesiologist clients grew, and his reputation for superior service and performance grew, those clients took pride in their role in making it happen. Everyone wants to be part of something vital. Leverage that natural impulse and get your clients on the team.

Tony also mentioned Larry Biederman and his SMART Marketing processes. It's good stuff from a great guy. Larry was with us as we introduced Supernova for the first time to a room full of people. Richard Weylman joined us soon after, and was a forceful presence onstage as we took Supernova from district to district. It was essential that we had acquisition experts with us to help drive the message that Supernova was about growth, not just folders.

Go find Richard's and Larry's work on acquisition and explore it, as well as Bill Cates's entire referral process. There's a lot of brilliance in the Supernova universe. There's also a lot of junk.

So find what is consistent with the tenets of Supernova and your practice, and then do it well. Okay, one more referral strategy.

Failure Point Analysis

Reason 4: Failure to Use Available Time for Growth

Unstructured time must take form. And the form it must take the majority of the time is on acquisition. Developing new business, either by referrals or by market positioning, is a major time commitment. Supernova creates the time, but it doesn't create the growth. You do. Failure here is harder to see right away because a lack of growth can hide a long time behind client satisfaction. But Supernova is a growth model, and it thrives only when it is growing.

Professional Networking at Supernova Speed

The concept of professional networking came from an internal training team at Merrill, and it's fabulous. It's been in play just a few years, and it's already helped some of our teams nearly double their assets under management.

Every Supernova advisor knows who else is on their client's financial team. They no doubt swap calls and documents with the CPA and the estate-planning attorney. So maybe it's time you really got to know them.

Next time you're meeting with a client, ask them, "Can you enthusiastically recommend your CPA?" They'll answer yes or no, and both are the right answers. Here's why:

Yes! They're accounting wizards who cast beautiful spells over our taxes.

Excellent. Let's meet them. We need to know who the best CPAs in town are because our other clients should be working with the best. Can you introduce us?

No. They're clods who couldn't find a deduction in a family of 12.

Let us help you, then. We know three CPAs who would be a good fit for you. Let us help you qualify them. We'll bring them in to meet you and then you can decide.

Add Up the Access and Goodwill

It's hard to count all the good things that can happen in each of the scenarios above. If they love their CPA, your meeting will be about deepening the financial team by solidifying the collaboration. When the CPA sees inside your service model (because you will tell them) and when they see how committed you are to true client-centered collaboration, they can recommend you fearlessly. You're not going to drag that client away from the CPA; in fact, you might bring them more business.

Add it up: You'll be doing even better for an important client; you connected with another resource for the rest of your clients; and you now have an inside position with a strong referring professional.

If your client can't enthusiastically recommend their CPA, rescue them. Set presentation appointments with your three favorite CPAs and help them find the right match. Along the way, you'll be creating goodwill for everyone in the room. The client gets great service and a CPA upgrade. The winning firm gets a new client and has a lot of love for you. Even the second- and third-place finishers will see you as a referral source and a service superstar.

Your Rolodex Is Starting to Glow

There is immense value in being a go-to guy when it comes to other professional resources. When you professionally network at Supernova speed, you simply grow the list of reputable and prospecting contacts that you can add to your Golden Rolodex. You also become the mavens that Malcolm Gladwell spoke so accurately and intuitively about in *The Tipping Point* (Little, Brown and Company, 2000). Mavens are the information gatherers within a network. They evaluate the messages that move through the network, and they pass their evaluations onto others. Mavens are powerful. Mavens are trusted. Supernova advisors who are creating exceptional growth are probably also mavens.

Let's move on quickly because I can hear the rising chorus of objections that's been getting louder in your head.

Who Has the Time?

Here's where two of the Supernova stars come into spectacular alignment: organization and acquisition.

Organization makes acquisition possible because it enforces essential rituals, be they client calls or business development. Organization creates time to prospect for potential clients and—even more importantly—protects that time against the creeping inefficiencies of a dynamic practice.

Even for a tried-and-true hunter or when you have a referral lead to follow up on, it's not always easy to pick up the phone and make the call. As soon as you put it on the list, the rest of the day will gobble it up. A Supernova advisor doesn't let it. He or she schedules time for acquisition efforts just as consistently as items on the 12/4/2 contact map. How much time? Well, how much do you want to grow?

Growth Goals Equal Time Spent on Growth

Tom Buck, a fantastic Supernova FA has a consistent goal of 20 percent growth a year. He reaches it because he consistently devotes 20 percent of his time—a full day each week—to marketing, prospecting, referral follow-up, and presentations.

He asks, "How can you expect to grow your business significantly and consistently without making growth a significant and continuing part of your weekly actions?" You can't, but many advisors try, just like Luke Skywalker *tried* to lift his ship using the force.

"Do not try. Do," said Yoda.

Develop your referral process. Position yourself in a market. Be a maven. Schedule the time. Grow.

Leaps

Practice

Harvesting referrals is an acquired skill. Hold role-playing sessions with your team. It might feel awkward and uncomfortable at first, but it leads to comfort, and then to mastery of the message. Then try it first on clients you're most comfortable with.

Ask

Are you referable? Really? Do an anonymous survey through a third party. Contemporary brand wisdom says your brand is not what you say it is; it's what customers say you are—the place you occupy in their universe. Brands that know where they're located in their customer's world, then occupy that space elegantly, are the winners. Find out. Claim it. Own it.

Align

The CPA example above is one sector you can align with. Also, consider attorneys, estate planners, even home builders and architects. Supernova is a model built on *interdependence.* Take it out to the business community and watch what it can do.

CHAPTER 7

Leading the Practice

LEADERS DEVELOPING LEADERS

In This Chapter

- Supernova leaders serve and develop their team.
- Leaders are change agents. If the team is not changing, the leader is not leading.
- Everything you want to accomplish, and everything you want your team to accomplish, can be broken down into small steps.
- Know those steps, post them, and track them for the entire team to see. Some teams call it a game board.
- Make every day a performance review for the team—constant feedback is the missing link for motivation.
- Share leadership: Empower your team. Expect accountability.

The leaders within the leadership star are every member of the team. Supernova creates transparent roles and responsibilities, and divides leadership among the entire team.

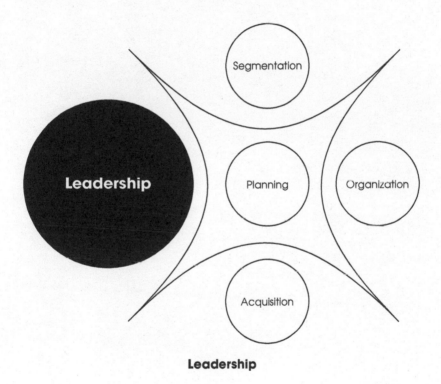

Leadership

In case you missed it so far, Supernova is a service model that creates growth. That doesn't change as we move into the fifth star, leadership. Leadership *is* service and it creates growth, both professionally and personally. Of course, putting service and leadership together in the same sentence is nothing new. You've no doubt heard the term *servant leadership*. You may have seen it in practice. Or have you?

In its most mature form, servant leadership is almost unrecognizable. That's because servant leaders have blended the practice of it so elegantly into the day-to-day business that it has become like spoken haikus from the haiku masters of ancient Japan. These masters would judge the success of their own haikus by their initial invisibility. If a haiku could be uttered in conversation with other haiku masters, and only later be recognized as a haiku, it had succeeded. True servant leadership is like this—that is, evident to perceptive people and seamlessly effective. This chapter is about making leadership more visible.

In 1970, Robert Greenleaf, a former AT&T manager turned cultural researcher, penned a small essay titled *The Servant as Leader* (available today through the Robert K. Greenleaf Center). As the 1960s grew increasingly tumultuous, Greenleaf tried to understand why so many young people were rebelling and rejecting America's institutions, especially colleges and universities. He concluded that it wasn't "kids these days"; instead, it was their leaders. Specifically, institutions were doing a poor job of serving young people. Translation: They were doing a poor job of leading. This insight shaped the rest of his career and inspired a bookshelf of titles from Stephen Covey to Ken Blanchard to a mentor of mine, Larry Wilson.

Larry calls his brand of leading *developmental leadership*. It's servant leadership in practice. Larry maintains that helping your colleagues grow and develop is a high form of service and leadership. He explains, "Some leaders believe their main job is to get *work done through people*. Other leaders believe their main job is to *get people done through work*. The first group wields fear in a command and control model. The second creates trust in a developmental environment."

Developmental leadership breathes new life into the old line about "people being our most important asset." While this phrase is true in many organizations, it's rarely the ultimate truth to the people charged with leading. It's also why so many organizations struggle with keeping their best people. When staff quit, they're not leaving the organization; they're leaving their bosses. Worse even is when they quit working but stay. Both environments are inefficient and fear laden. They make it hard for a business to grow and staff to develop because they are nearly impossible to change. And all effective leaders, no matter what type of leadership they model, are agents of change.

The Best Meeting We've Ever Been To

You remember Chris Brooke and Rita McCluskey from Chapter 5. They do so many things right. In fact, they are one of the most successful groups in implementing the five stars of Supernova in their purest form. They have taught me much, including one of the best ways to take a meeting.

They stand.

Yes, they do have a conference table and chairs, and they use both often. Just not for their 11:00 session.

They gather around a CA's desk or in an office, each taking their turn talking about what they need to do today and what they need from the team to get it done. The whole thing is over by the time most meetings get everyone at the table with their freshened-up coffee.

It's also beautifully named. They simply called it the "stand-up." What better way to say we own this business together and we are standing up to the challenge of running it together.

It's a winner. Try it.

Three Reasons to Change

Crisis

As you've read in the earlier chapters, our teams at Merrill changed their business model because we were in crisis. Financial Advisors (FAs) were endlessly trying to meet the demands of numerous clients, who in turn felt they were not being advised or served adequately. Essentially, crises such as these are the early signs of an organization that must change. We've learned enough about change since then to know that there are two other reasons to change: evolution and anticipation.

Evolution

Teams also change when their leaders help them see that things all around them are changing. In order to survive these changes, it is necessary that they adapt and evolve. We call this concept "Darwinism Meets Financial Services." In other words, the need to evolve is what's propelling the change.

Leading an evolutionary change requires a deft touch. It's instinctive for team members to view a changing environment as a fearful place. Fear focused externally will become internalized to the same degree that leaders use fear to manage their team. Those teams will be essentially frozen in the oncoming headlights until the changing environment collides with them hard enough to create a full-blown crisis. What happens after that determines their future. Ah yes, the future. . . .

Anticipation

Anticipatory change involves the uncertain science and intuitive art of envisioning the future and then changing ahead of it. The stated goal, of course, is to thrive once it arrives. The problem is the future never does quite arrive; it's always out there. And the environment you envisioned, no matter how uncanny your singular predictions, will have complexities unseen even in your crystal ball. We've seen it firsthand.

Our leadership teams at Merrill were continually looking for cues on how to change in anticipation. We dove with confidence into the sea of change as we anticipated the importance of consulting and advising versus just selling. We saw that future clearly, or so we thought. We embraced anticipatory change and we became very confident in our abilities to not just stay ahead of the curve, but to ride it, steer it, and make it go our way. It was our "pride before the fall" moment.

We were preparing for a relatively narrow vision of the future when another more complex and unstable one dawned. We had not anticipated the full consequences of our bloated books and the reactions of our poorly served clients. Anticipating change successfully in some areas (the importance of consulting versus selling) had not shielded us from a crisis (the consequences of bloated books) that demanded a deeper and more lasting change.

So the challenge to leaders who are leading anticipatory change is to *thrive now while changing to thrive in the clearest future you can envision.* Sounds easy, right? It's not, but it's what true leaders do.

Let's move back into the workday of a Supernova team and explore some of the leadership principles they bring to life. Each tenet has a utility for you as you lead your team, whether you are in crisis, evolving, or anticipating a new environment. They each express an aspect of developmental leadership.

These principles make everyone on the team a leader by cultivating accountability that is equal parts reflection and ownership. It's about shared responsibility. And it begins with the little things, all spelled out in black and red.

Lessons from the Nation's Best Dental Practice

Darby Henley, a former sales manager at Merrill Lynch, was there at the creation of Supernova. Along with Jim Walker and Jeff Ransdell, Darby articulated what we were all sensing about the model after we had started to see it perform: "Segmentation, organization, and acquisition each deliver their own kind of jolt to the system, and that's good, but to be successful over time they need something to tie them together."

Darby, you see, had an idea. It was something he had seen in his father-in-law's dental practice, which was unlike any other practice in the United States. It had been recognized by a panel of his peers evaluating the business side of the dental business. They tagged it "the most productive dental practice in America."

As mentioned in Chapter 4, a dental office surprisingly operates in a similar fashion to an FA's office that implements the Supernova. Like an FA, a dentist makes money when his or her time is focused on patients or clients—not cleaning teeth, not scheduling the next appointment, not taking x-rays. And it's the same for a Supernova practice.

Darby's father-in-law had mastered the art and science of keeping the most patients possible in the chairs and keeping the dentists focused exclusively on treating those patients with the highest-value services. So did the guy just have fast hands and uber-aggressive scheduling? No. He had a gameboard.

Break It Down, Put It Up

The gameboard was a poster that listed everyone in the dental practice and their quantifiable task goals for the week, stuff like "make 50 appointments" or "create 15 new client folders." Then, when the scheduler hit the goal, or exceeded it, they wrote the number in black. If the scheduler did not hit the goal, then the actual number was written in red. Boom. Right there, for all to see—a poster that listed the collective productivity of each member of the practice.

The gameboard allowed everyone to know who was hitting their goals, who was not, and who might need some help. Consistently hitting or exceeding a goal was a clear sign of increasing efficiency and productivity, and demonstrated that the staff member was ready to reach a higher goal. Consistently missed goals were a sign that the person needed momentary help. Other times, it indicated that the goal was out of line with their role or ability and consequently led to a change in their original job responsibilities.

The result of this system was steady growth in practice productivity (profitability tracked right along with it, too). The transparent nature of responsibilities gave everyone clear ownership of their role. What they did with that ownership says as much about the effectiveness of the system as it does about the culture of the practice.

The practice was alive with camaraderie. Support and friendly competition worked hand in hand. Good work went recognized without a single "this job is soooo hard and I'm so essential to it" sigh.

What's more, Darby's father-in-law didn't start out calling it the "gameboard." His staff gave it the name, and it reflected their approach. It wasn't the "public shame board" or the "relative merit" board, although it might have been in less evolved settings. In this practice, people carried their work lightly and still took it seriously.

Why the Gameboard Works

I'm giving this a lot of ink here because Darby preached it to us with the fervor of a believer. "And the best part," he said, "was that the practice managed itself. My father-in-law is a dentist, not a general. He hates telling people how to do their jobs."

Beautiful. Stuff got done. People got better. People had fun. The practice grew. So we decided to field-test it in our Supernova world.

It doesn't matter if your investment model is visionary or if new clients are throwing their millions your way every week. If your practice doesn't have a gameboard or the blocking and tackling down cold, nothing works.

Don't be overly taken by Supernova's promise of exceptional service or the slap-your-forehead appropriateness of the 12/4/2 contact ritual, or even the powerful simplicity of the client folders. None of it is self-created. It all takes work. And all work can be broken down into component pieces. So go get an easel and some markers, and let's make one of those gameboards.

12/4/2 Works Inside the Team, Too

The Supernova contact ritual can create exceptional experiences for your clients *and your team*. What would happen if you had time scheduled every month with each member of the team? Not to talk about specific work issues, but to talk about the team members, their careers, their professional goals? What if four of those meetings were about setting specific goals for the quarter? What if two of them were deep talks that touched all the bases in that person's life?

What happens is this: The team member is engaged at levels far more meaningful than an annual review or the pat on the back at the holiday party. They are heard and seen in ways most supervisors simply don't have time for. Supernova makes the time. Use it to make your team better.

The Supernova Gameboard

In order to create the Supernova gameboard, let's first start with the part of a practice everyone owns: service. At the task level, what makes service exceptional? Regularly scheduled contact, for one. So break scheduled contact down into tasks like setting appointments and confirming appointments. Remember, 12/4/2 means monthly calls, quarterly reviews, and biannual planning sessions. In order to set the baseline goals for the players on the gameboard, think of the kind of contact, the number of clients, and the FA's time capacity to make a call or a meeting. Let's say that's 30 contacts per FA.

Based on that thinking, let's also say that the CA has a weekly goal of 20 appointments. She has other things to do, obviously, and not all of them can be quantified. Or can they? One problem we see with underperforming practices (or people) is that they continually fail to see their larger objectives as a series of small steps. They procrastinate. They do more research. They do whatever they do that keeps them from accomplishing significant objectives.

So break it down, and let small successes grow. That's shopworn advice. And yet, if you don't believe it and act on it, then your practice will never reach the potential that Supernova reveals.

The Engaged Person

Supernova teams are comprised of people who are fully engaged. This chapter discusses how leadership creates that engagement. In his business handbook *Propel Frontline Leaders*, George Reavis presents this snapshot of the engaged person:

- People demonstrate their intentions. They commit themselves.
- People are reflective. They continuously learn.
- People pay attention. They are focused.

Source: George Reavis, *Propel Frontline Leaders*, 2005.

Back to your gameboard.

So what can't be broken down to smaller goals in a Supernova practice? Assume that everything can, and try. Acquisition can. Acquisition is about several things, like asking for advice on how to grow. It's a great idea, and you are absolutely going to do it when the time is right with the right client, right? Wrong. Set a weekly goal and track it. Even two or three may be plenty.

Referral calls are another activity that can easily be broken down: let's say five a week, and maybe one meeting per week. And this occurs throughout the practice until everyone has a few quantified goals for the week. Now write them on a presentation pad and put them in the conference room or an FA's office—just not the broom closet, because this thing needs fresh air to thrive. People have to see it, touch it, interact with it, reflect on it. Yes, reflect.

Reflective Accountability

Reflective accountability is a term you probably haven't heard before. We hadn't until work on this book began and we went looking for a way to describe the personal experience of having a gameboard within a Supernova practice. Reflective accountability was where we landed and it works.

Accountability arrives preloaded with meaning: responsibility, maturity, integrity, and so on. Accountability is good, and more is better.

Reflection is how accountability grows, collectively and individually. No one can force a person to reflect on his or her performance (ask any parent of teenagers). It's self-generated, and it helps if the generator is continually on. That's what the public posting of the gameboard goals does. It fosters an internal environment of reflection: Am I working as hard as I can to reach these goals? Do they accurately reflect my values? Should I ask for help? Should I help someone else? Can I get better? It's what everyone in every organization should be asking. And there's no reason to keep the answers to themselves. . . .

Gather 'Round the Gameboard

This is where the concept comes full circle, bringing us back to a practice run by a whole group of leaders. Each week, call a quick meeting to review and discuss the gameboard.

> **Mr. Acquisition 1:** "Okay, as you can see, I did hit my goals in asking for advice and in making contact

	with referrals. Those are all going forward nicely and I'm pleased with what I accomplished."
Ms. Contact 1:	"I hit my numbers but don't feel great about the week. Some other things that should have gotten done, didn't, and I'm not sure why. "
Mr. Acquisition 2:	"What looks like a bad week for me up here was really a good one. Here's why. . . ."
Ms. Contact 2:	"Reached my goals by Thursday morning. Normal week."

All kinds of experiences, as you can imagine. Also, an opportunity for a kind of dialogue that is rare in organizations today.

All too often, the discussion of goals, met or not, is constrained within the employee/supervisor relationship. The performance evaluation has become a private conversation that at its best involves two people, and its worst involves one person talking and the other person listening. What does a team gain from that? Nothing.

By taking performance public on the gameboard, everyone else knows what the other members of the team are focusing on. That's infinitely more helpful than merely knowing their title or role and carrying around expectations of them that are vague or unspoken or just plain wrong.

Failure Point Analysis

Reason 5: Poor Accountability

Poor accountability is a cultural issue that challenges even the highest performers. They often confuse accountability with perfection. Perfection is impossible to obtain and sustain, and exhausting to try. Perfectionism is just another kind of dysfunction. And Supernova can cure it, too. Supernova accountability doesn't demand perfection. Rather, it compels ownership. Make a mistake? Own it. Have a bad week? Claim it, talk about it, share the frustration. Accountability is a commitment everyone makes and everyone talks about. Perfectionism is a personal problem that drags the team into it. Let it go, and keep talking about improving.

With publicly posted goals, improvement opportunities are revealed in real time, and with an explicit invitation for group-generated problem solving. Maybe that role isn't right for that person, so talk about where they fit better. Maybe the acquisition part of the business is bringing in too much and you're drifting back into the craziness.

Accountability and reflection—this way of working creates a clear vision of what a successful week looks like. Imagine the power of that. It is literally transformative. It alters how a team thinks and talks to itself. Asking a critical question such as "How are we doing?" is the missing link in motivation and engagement. It's how the brilliance of Supernova is sustained. And it is nothing more than small goals written on a big sheet.

Let's move on, or actually back to where I began the chapter: leadership and change.

> It is difficult for people to stay absorbed in any activity unless they get timely information about how well they are doing. Feedback may come from colleagues or supervisors but preferably the activity itself will provide the feedback. The ability to give oneself objective feedback to oneself is in fact the mark of an expert.
>
> Mihaly Csikszentmihalyi
> *Source: Good Business: Leadership, Flow, and the Making of Meaning, and Flow: The Psychology of Optimal Experience* (Harper & Row, 1990): 143.

Why People Change

Brilliant strategists can be ineffective leaders, and a bold leader can lead a team right over the cliff. These brands of leadership usually share the same default setting—they command and control and use fear to motivate. Fear can motivate, briefly and haphazardly. It never inspires. Fear works against high performance, and Supernova *is* high performance.

We're not the first people to recognize fear as a drag on change. W. Edwards Deming, the World War II–era quality guru knew that fear hampered effectiveness. In his now-famous 14 Points (see sidebar), he states it clearly in Point 8: Drive out fear and build trust so that everyone can work more effectively. The full collection reads like a wish list for every servant leader, but Deming himself said that if number 8 isn't implemented, the other 13 points *won't work*. That moves it up to number 1 in a Supernova team. Drive out fear and build trust.

The processes we've explored in this chapter—reflection, accountability, shared responsibility, and engagement—all sync up to reduce fear and build trust.

Deming's 14 Points

Deming defined 14 key principles for leaders to master when transforming their business:

1. Create constancy of purpose for the improvement of products and services, with the aim to become competitive, stay in business, and provide jobs.
2. Adopt a new philosophy of cooperation (win-win) in which everybody wins and put it into practice by teaching it to employees, customers, and suppliers.
3. Cease dependence on mass inspection to achieve quality. Instead, improve the process and build quality into the product in the first place.
4. End the practice of awarding business on the basis of price tag alone. Instead, minimize total cost in the long run. Move toward a single supplier for any one item, based on a long-term relationship of loyalty and trust.
5. Improve constantly, and forever, the system of production, service, and planning of any activity. This will improve quality and productivity and thus constantly decrease costs.
6. Institute training for skills.

7. Adopt and institute leadership for the management of people, recognizing their different abilities, capabilities, and aspirations. The aim of leadership should be to help people, machines, and gadgets do a better job. Leadership of management is in need of an overhaul, as well as leadership of production workers.
8. Drive out fear and build trust so that everyone can work more effectively.
9. Break down barriers between departments. Abolish competition and build a win-win system of cooperation within the organization. People in research, design, sales, and production must work as a team to foresee problems of production and use that might be encountered with the product or service.
10. Eliminate slogans, exhortations, and targets asking for zero defects or new levels of productivity. Such exhortations only create adversarial relationships, as the bulk of the causes of low quality and low productivity belong to the system and thus lie beyond the power of the workforce.
11. Eliminate numerical goals, numerical quotas, and management by objectives. Substitute leadership.
12. Remove barriers that rob people of joy in their work. This will mean abolishing the annual rating or merit system that ranks people and creates competition and conflict.
13. Institute a vigorous program of education and self-improvement.
14. Put everybody in the company to work to accomplish the transformation. The transformation is everybody's job.

Source: W. Edwards Deming, *Out of the Crisis,* Washington, D.C.: Edwards Deming Institute, 1986.

The Bank of Trust, Internal Branch

We introduced you to the Bank of Trust in Chapter 4. There's a branch of trust inside every team, too, and deposits into it strengthen the platform from which leaders lead. Leaders need to be trusted; team members need to trust each other; leaders need to trust the team. And everyone needs to trust that the change under way is the right thing to do. Keeping trust alive and well is the biggest challenge for any leader, Supernova included. Why?

Preserving trust in the midst of change is not an intellectual challenge, it's an emotional challenge. American business leaders too often demand that emotions be left at home. In their eyes, emotions are suspect and even irrelevant. How absurd and, ultimately, unproductive.

Try this: Read each statement below and decide which one is more emotionally accurate.

I think I can trust him.

I feel I can trust him.

I trust him.

The first statement is uneasy with itself because trust exists somewhere south of the brain, in the heart and the gut. The second statement gets closer to emotional accuracy because it exists in the realm of emotion. The third statement possesses the gravity of experience and probably feels the most authentic. That's because trust is emotion fed by experience. What we do as leaders is the experience that informs the emotions of your team.

When people resist change, they often agree with the dynamic merits intellectually. It's their emotional state that keeps them stuck. Intellectually, they agree with you, but emotionally, they don't. They are literally victims of unconscious responses to what's happening at that moment. The best leaders understand the undercurrent of emotional resistance, and they guide people to change for their own reasons, not the leader's. In these moments, the change gets a new owner, and the shift in ownership is what activates Supernova's transformative energy.

Who's the Boss?

Giving people a reason to change that resonates emotionally requires letting go of traditional leadership behaviors and sharing leadership with the entire team. High-performance

Supernova teams cultivate individual leaders by sharing ownership in highly specific terms. We've heard this: "The CAs are in charge of all client coordination and communication." Okay, now what happens if something gets dropped or if a client leaves? Lots of finger pointing because no one owned anything exclusively.

A better way to avoid finger pointing is to assign sets of clients to individual CAs so that they are the lead CA on their piece of the business. They are supported by the rest of the team, but they *own* the relationships. Watch what happens when a problem arrives, as they always do. If there's any finger pointing, it will probably point back to the pointer. And that person has probably already developed and implemented an effective response. Ownership becomes leadership. And the team becomes stronger.

Listening: A Primer

"To learn from people, you have to listen to them with respect. (It is) not as easy as you might imagine. . . . The trouble with listening for many of us Is that while we're supposedly doing it, we're actually busy composing what we're going to say next. . . . (During) your next personal encounter, try to employ the tactics we've outlined here:

- Listen.
- Don't interrupt.
- Don't finish the other person's sentences.
- Don't say "I knew that."
- Don't even agree with the other person (even if he praises you, just say, "Thank you").
- Don't use the words "no," "but," and "however."
- Don't be distracted. Don't let your eyes or attention wander elsewhere while the other person is talking.
- Maintain your end of the dialogue by asking questions that either:
  - Show you are paying attention.

(Continued)

> - Move the dialogue forward.
> - Require the other person to talk (while you listen).
> - Eliminate any striving to impress the other person with how smart or funny you are. . . .
>
> (You will learn, and as an ancillary benefit) you'll uncover a glaring paradox: The more you subsume your desire to shine (and truly listen), the more you will shine in the other person's eyes."
>
> Source: Marshall Goldsmith, *What Got You Here Won't Get You There*, Hyperion, 2007 pp. 148–156.

Do More with Less—Really

In the introduction, you read how Supernova was created through the perfect storm of poor service, overworked staffs, and client defections. You've seen how Supernova helped right each of those wrongs, yet you might not have noticed that we still haven't hired anyone to help.

Supernova works with small teams. Small teams can drive growth without adding to the workload or the stress. Remember, growth in a Supernova practice is about managing the min/max balance precisely. The client list stays about the same so the service demands are only going to fluctuate within the range of current client needs. We've seen Supernova teams grow their assets under management by 200 percent, 300 percent, and more without a single new employee.

That's not to say that the team adopting Supernova is always the right team to succeed within it. A Supernova team depends on people who are willing and able to lead their share of it. If they are neither, they need to leave. As the saying goes, if you can't change the people, you have to change the people. When a model like Supernova disrupts the traditional (and typically dysfunctional) ways of working, then what we expect from our people and from ourselves has to endure disruption.

Five Essential Actions

More from George Reavis and *Propel Frontline Leaders*. In his business model, Reavis speaks about how leaders must continually align the goals of the team with the frontline behaviors to get them done. He identifies five actions:

1. **Thank**: Builds recognition and leads appreciation.
2. **Invite**: Demonstrates intentions, which leads to commitments.
3. **Ask critical questions**: Creates attention and leads to long-term focus.
4. **Get feedback from activities**: Keeps associates engaged at a high level.
5. **Share assessments**: Develops opinions that foster dialogue.

Source: George Reavis, *Propel Frontline Leaders*, 2005

Implementation Is Experimentation

Supernova was created through small-scale experimentation and evaluation. In one group, we segmented the book but nothing more. And nothing much happened. In another group we tried to implement 12/4/2 on a big hairy book, and it bit back. With another team, we put an acquisition model in place that whiffed because the group's service simply hadn't earned them the right to be referred.

We worked our way to a high confidence level because we took a leap of faith and stepped on that well-supported bridge. When we took Supernova on the road, we knew it worked and why. We had piloted it numerous ways in numerous teams.

Trust that's vital to change grows slowly, so implement slowly. Pilot before you roll out, and if possible, do multiple pilots. Discoveries are rarely the product of answering a single question. They come from circling a problem a couple of ways, asking the same questions about dissimilar experiments, and seeing what you collect.

It's another way to spread the leadership, too. Let people participate in a pilot in meaningful ways. Ownership is investment, and investors—you might have heard—like to see their investments succeed.

Drive out fear. Build trust. Share leadership. Succeed.

Leaps

Did You Do Your Job Today?

Are you sure? Did you really know what today was meant to accomplish? Realistic goals and a laser beam focus are what make productive, satisfying days. Try it and see how you feel.

The Power of Promising

A public promise, to stop smoking or to call 10 clients, can be a strong motivator. Make a commitment to your team and ask them to do the same. Write it down, post it, and track it. Compare that to other commitments made in the past that simply evaporated under the pressures of work or the accumulation of time.

See It, Own It, Solve It

Leadership is more than power and control. It's keen observation, clear communication, and problem solving. What do you see on your team that you can take sole responsibility for making better? It's not doing another's job or "blame-storming." It's getting involved and being clear about what you're trying to accomplish. That's leadership, without the corner office to certify it.

12/4/2 Your World

You've read about the Supernova contact ritual for your clients and your team. Who else? Try everyone in the relationship—the CPA, the estate planner, the insurance agent. Model for them what exceptional service looks like by bringing them into the contact ritual of monthly, scheduled calls. Think about what you can learn and what you can bring to *every client relationship* when you are deepening your knowledge this way.

Final Thoughts on Moving Forward

As you think about what this book has revealed to you, and consider how to take your own leap toward creating the ultimate client experience, I suggest that you journey backward through the book.

Leadership: Leadership is where you should begin your quest to exceptional client service and consistent growth because it's the most important factor in the success of a team. Remember, it's not leadership with a capital *L;* rather, it's creating leaders within a practice and developing them to be their best. In other words, it's servant leadership.

Acquisition: You didn't need me to tell you about the importance of referrals. You probably already have a business development strategy. Acquiring new clients may be the most active component of your business. Just make sure it's also the most integrated. Acquisition is a tempting pick for the brightest star in Supernova and appears to be the place to focus your energies. Success in acquiring new relationships is only as meaningful as the success of the planning and the effectiveness of the leadership within the team. That's why focusing on growth, as opposed to serving clients, undercuts your team's values. Once a team puts its needs—faster growth, more clients, higher fees—ahead of its clients, it loses its soul. And it can happen in subtle ways, without anyone even noticing.

Planning: Planning in its most intimate and integrated form is the next step you must take on the bridge. It's service; it's compassion; it's respect. It's what a financial advisor has to sell, regardless of what's in the brochure.

Organization: Organization matters the way gauges matter to a pilot. You can fly without them, but if you chose to do so, you've cut your effectiveness as a pilot down to nearly zero. There's a crash looming for the FA who eschews organization.

Segmentation: Segmentation is the first essential step across the bridge, but it doesn't need to be coached—it needs to be evaluated, planned, and executed. If the 80/20 Rule has exceptions, we've not seen them. Segment and get smaller, so that you can serve and get better.

The invisible bridge has now been built and defined. As you have read this book, you have walked across this amazing structure in your mind. You've imagined the journey, and, like so many journeys, this one has delivered you back to where it all began: trust.

For Indiana Jones to step onto a bridge that wasn't visible, he needed to trust it would be there. For you to take the first step toward practicing the principles of Supernova, and the next, and the next, you must return to trust.

Trust the people who have implemented the phases of Supernova and the people who are on the Supernova journey with you now. Trust your team to rise up and become leaders. Trust yourself. Trust this journey.

And remember the old knight's words—**choose wisely**. . . . The immortal knight knows about the internal and external dilemmas you encounter as you reach for a new business opportunity, or pursue a client, or consider a new way to run your business. He knows that the unwise choices outnumber the wise choice by a large margin. He also knows that after making it this far, you are not going to simply admire the grails, compliment him on his longevity, and go back the way you came. For many of you, going back to an overabundance of clients is not an option. You have a choice to make, so make one that better serves your clients and brings meaning to your work and your life.

There are challenges ahead. Skeptics are everywhere, which can be a good thing. Encourage skepticism as much as enthusiasm. After all, these two emotions often come from the same place—the gut. That's where instincts seem to reside, and these instincts are powerful determinants of human behavior.

When we rolled out Supernova, we welcomed the skeptics and encouraged them to question their existing practices by engaging them in the 80/20 Rule point by point. These groups that challenged Supernova were often the teams that ultimately did the best with it. That's because they understood that untested ideas, no matter how compelling, were simply untested ideas. And the testing begins with the sharp questions. So ask tough questions, of yourself, of your team, of me.

Viktor Frankl, the holocaust survivor who wrote the landmark book on existential psychology entitled *Man's Search for Meaning* (Washington Square Press, 1967), once said, "What gives light must endure heat" (p. 157).

Indeed.

Supernova is a light that has endured the heat, from a change-averse corporate culture to a sudden and ruthless bear market. It has radiated across the careers of thousands of financial advisors and continues to do so.

Supernova has given the fire in my belly something to illuminate. I care deeply about serving people and propelling them to their potential. Supernova is what allowed me to serve in a meaningful and measurable way, and Supernova has served me as well. It was the gift given to me by the extraordinary people who helped create it. And now, it's yours.

About the Author

Rob Knapp is a native of Massachusetts and a 1968 graduate of Wake Forest, where he both played and coached tennis. In 1969 he joined the U.S. Navy and became a pilot. He flew and trained on the Navy's fleet of F-4s, OV-10s, P-3s, S-2s, and several helicopters. His passion for coaching top performers was born on the courts and in the cockpit. In 1972 he joined Merrill Lynch and following seven years as a Financial Advisor (FA) in Boston, he was given the chance to coach again, as a sales manager in Merrill's Chicago office. He eventually rose to the position of District Director, one of 14 at the time within Merrill Lynch. He retired in 2006 as Managing Director of Merrill Lynch's Indiana operations.

At Merrill, Knapp was widely recognized as an innovator and, occasionally, an iconoclast. He put the long-term development of his teams ahead of short-term gains, and those people are now some of the most successful FA teams in the company. His former managers are consistently recognized for their accomplishments in developing teams, serving clients, and generating revenue.

Helping high performers reach even higher is a lifelong calling and his ongoing passion.

Supernova Consulting Group

After retirement from Merrill, Knapp founded the Supernova Consulting Group to work with teams, executive leadership, and entire organizations. Knapp's consulting practice mirrors his leadership approach at Merrill, which embodied professional development through personal accountability and creative experimentation. Knapp helps people create and sustain highly productive environments that engender trust and reject fear.

Learn more at www.supernovaconsulting.com.

Supporting the Knapp Scholars

One hundred percent of the author's proceeds from the sale of *The Supernova Advisor* will be used to fund college scholarships for deserving students in financial need. These Knapp Scholars will learn the tenants of servant leadership as they prepare for careers in business and financial service.

Index